Ethical Dilemmas in Justice Studies

By

Julie B. Raines

Ethical Dilemmas in Justice Studies

By Julie B. Raines

This book first published 2024

Ethics International Press Ltd, UK

British Library Cataloguing in Publication Data

A catalogue record for this book is available from the British Library

Print Book ISBN: 978-1-80441-342-5

eBook ISBN: 978-1-80441-343-2

Table of Contents

List of Tables

Foreword

Across many countries, public confidence in the institutions of justice is trending downward. Annual surveys conducted by the Gallup organization in the United States show a citizenry with little faith in the police, Supreme Court, and criminal justice system. Growing mistrust in the police, courts, and corrections knows no borders. Negative perceptions of the justice system are endemic across certain groups, especially those who are disproportionately targeted for arrest or too poor to mount an effective legal defense. The growing trust deficit between the justice system and community members is worrisome on many levels. Individuals who question the validity and fairness of the justice system are much less likely to abide by it. Why conform to the rule of law when it is applied unequally across the population? Declining confidence in justice institutions also has the effect of hardening the lines that already separate peoples according to race, economics, and country of origin. Under these circumstances, good governance and the maintenance of civil society are less assured and regimes become more unstable.

The antecedents for growing mistrust are complex and varied. Citizens are reporting less support for all types of civil institutions – both public to private – from political parties to organized religion. There is likely some connection between lower trust in institutions more generally and justice institutions in particular. Changing political understandings about the role of government in society and perhaps even generational issues may be influencing faith in government. However, there are many instances where the misbehavior of justice system actors contributes to its poor standing with the public. The world witnessed the murder of George Floyd as he struggled for breath under the knee of a Minneapolis police officer along a busy thoroughfare. Pictures of the violent and dehumanizing tactics used by guards at Abu Ghraib prison in Iraq are still widely circulated. Recent revelations about U.S. Supreme Court Justice Clarence Thomas' receipt of lavish gifts and vacations add to the sense that justice can be bought for the right price. In many ways, these are self-inflicted wounds perpetrated on the justice system by the actors themselves.

So, how does one rebuild confidence in the institutions of justice? The solution largely rests in the age-old question inherent in democratic political systems -- how to keep government officials accountable to the citizenry and their elected representatives. Governments may coax law-abiding, public-spirited behavior from its justice system actors through a host of formal tools including legislative inquiries, transparency rules, and citizen oversight bodies. These are of limited effect without a complementary focus on the informal means of promoting integrity and fairness in official behavior.

This is the space that *Ethical Dilemmas in Justice Studies* seeks to fill. Taking an applied approach to ethics, the text offers an invitation to students and practitioners alike to anticipate the types of ethical questions they will face in the workplace. The book is peppered with numerous case studies and debate topics across all justice contexts to accomplish this purpose. The approach used by Julie Raines aligns with a sentiment expressed in Rosemary O'Leary's important book *The Ethics of Dissent*, "ethics is not a spectator sport—it is a contact sport" (p. 16). The idea is to study and debate complex ethical dilemmas *before* experiencing them in a professional setting. It is like any task in life, the more one practices, the better the results. This holds true whether the task is target shooting, solving a math problem, or navigating an ethical dilemma. In short, we cannot simply wait for someone else to tell us the right course, we must be proactive in searching out ethical questions and applying appropriate ethical reasoning.

The reader is encouraged to accept Raines' invitation to wrestle with the complex ethical questions she throws our way. By doing so, you not only contribute to the fair and equal administration of justice but help to rally public confidence in the institutions of justice.

James R. Brunet
North Carolina State University
December 2023

Reference

O'Leary, Rosemary. (2006). *The Ethics of Dissent: Managing Guerrilla Government*. Washington, DC: CQ Press

Chapter 1
Morality and Ethics

Chapter Objectives

1. Define the concepts of morality, ethics, values, duties, moral dilemmas, and whistleblowing.
2. Identify conflicting values and duties and how these conflicts develop into moral/ethical dilemmas.
3. Examine moral/ethical dilemmas and how to approach these dilemmas.

Introduction

Every Harry Potter fan can probably recite for you the tale of the three brothers as written by Beedle the Bard. It is a parable of sorts – a story that has several obvious moral lessons. Two of the three brothers try to cheat death and live forever which has negative consequences for both brothers. Their two stories highlight the dangers of wielding unbridled power, as well as the importance of accepting grief over the loss of a loved one. Each brother has a story that shows what they each value.

Parables can typically be found in religious stories which is not surprising since moral philosophy and religious philosophy, not to mention legal reasoning, are all tightly connected in many ways. While Harry Potter is not a religious story, it has the same elements found in most parables – life lessons when values and/or duties come into conflict. As moral/ethical dilemmas happen because of competing values and/or duties/obligations, this chapter then focuses on values, duties, obligations, and ethical dilemmas. This is followed by a discussion of whistleblowing and considerations in the ethical collection of both quantitative and qualitative data in criminal justice research. We begin, however, much more broadly looking at the concepts of morality and ethics.

Morality

Defining **morality** is complex, but most definitions include a behavioral code that rational, moral actors adhere to and endorse for the good of a larger group, namely society. **Morality** often also includes concepts of etiquette or small morals, religious morality, and legal or written behavioral codes (Gert & Gert, 2020). In the Harry Potter parable, the first brother uses an all-powerful magic wand to commit murder and then proceeds to boast about his invincibility. The first brother has violated both a legal and religious behavioral code of committing murder. He has also violated a religious moral code of boasting which is considered a sin of pride. Boasting could also arguably be considered a violation of etiquette as society does not generally approve of people who brag or boast.

We constantly judge whether human behavior is good or bad when determining whether behavior is moral or not. Some argue that we can't judge whether behavior is moral or not based on universal notions of moral behavior, but that **morality** is dependent on the individual themselves (also known as **moral relativism** where what is judged as good or bad conduct is determined by the individual), as well as the context, culture, and norms of the society they live in. Based on the first brother's behavior, we could judge his behavior to be bad or immoral, but according to moral relativism, the first brother may consider his own behavior morally justified which is one of the criticisms of **moral relativism**.

Our roles and status in society also determine how we are expected to act and contribute to how we are judged with respect to the morality of our behavior. I am a professor, and you are a student – these roles give us each certain levels of status within society. The expectations are that I will treat you in the way I treat other students, with expectations of completing assignments on time, and you will treat me the way you treat other professors, with expectations that I provide guidance throughout the semester on how to complete those assignments.

According to Socrates, bad behavior comes from ignorance or lack of knowledge and one can only achieve happiness by being virtuous which requires attaining knowledge. In the law, individuals who may have difficulty attaining knowledge measured by their IQ are often treated differently, excused from entering contracts, and spared from the death penalty. Aristotle, on the other hand, believed that bad behavior did not come from ignorance but from human weakness and that individuals who engage in bad behavior do so knowingly. This concept of "knowingly" also shows up in the law when determining a defendant's level of responsibility for committing a crime or culpability. An individual who is merely reckless, perhaps acting dangerously without realizing the potential consequences, is held to a lesser standard of culpability than someone who acts knowingly, whether they knew (actual knowledge) or should have known (constructive knowledge) their behavior would cause harm.

This brings us to the ultimate question – to whom does morality apply? Do we judge my dog on her behavior and whether it is moral or not? Philosophers agree that we look towards rational actors when judging morality and while I believe my dog to be quite brilliant, I would agree with philosophers that rational actors are generally limited to humans and their moral behavior. How we define rationality is a trickier question, however, but it's safe to say that morality applies to anyone who can understand what it means to be rational leaving out small children and individuals who have significant cognitive impairment.

Case 1.1: Morality
Mel Gibson is an actor and director who has battled alcoholism. While intoxicated on multiple occasions he has made appalling homophobic, antisemitic, and racist comments. Each time he said something despicable, he apologized, and eventually he entered rehabilitative treatment for his alcoholism. He was ultimately blacklisted by Hollywood for about 10 years. Does being moral mean never making mistakes? Does alcoholism excuse Mel's behavior? Is it possible to atone for such behavior? Was blacklisting him from his profession for 10 years an appropriate response?

Ethics

Morality and **ethics** are used interchangeably even though ethics is really the study of morality or what is judged to be good or bad behavior. **Meta-ethics** is the study of ethical systems and whether those systems follow the principles of moral relativism or a universalistic approach as with ethical formalism (which will be discussed in the next chapter). In this text, we examine **applied ethics** which focuses on a specific issue, our issue being the criminal justice system. We also examine several areas of **professional ethics**, which is a subset of **applied ethics**, including policing, courts, and corrections.

Normative ethics takes morality a step further by proposing how one should act and live, as well as what kind of person one should be and this is achieved by "stating and defending the most basic moral principles" (Kagan, 2018, p. 2). Figuring out what are the basic moral principles, rights, or duties is at the heart of normative ethics. For example, the first brother in the parable doesn't appear to have a moral justification for murdering another human being and harming another person is not considered a moral act except for rare circumstances such as self-defense or defense of others. Normative ethics would propose then that the first brother acted immorally under the circumstances.

Situational ethics, like **moral relativism**, takes an individualistic approach, but rather than solely focusing on the individual to determine morality, it focuses on the surrounding context of the moral dilemma. For example, the story of the first brother gives us no context regarding the dispute he had with the man he murders, nor does it give any context regarding his life in that moment. Would we judge the first brother differently if he had been wronged by the man he murdered? Or if he had recently endured terrible misfortunes leading up to his immoral behavior? These finer details give us the context we need to judge the first brother's behavior according to situational ethics.

Until this point, we've considered judging the morality of specific behavior, but we haven't considered what makes someone a moral or ethical person. The first brother's behavior is ultimately immoral according to most codes of conduct, but is he an immoral person negating all the good he may have accomplished up until that moment in his life? **Virtue ethics** is a system of normative ethics that focuses on an individual's character. Good character or **virtues** include wisdom, justice, courage, and temperance according to stoicism. Similarly, Aristotle defined virtues as wisdom, understanding, generosity, and self-control and that individuals can develop good habits to flourish and achieve happiness. The other two systems of ethics, which focus on behavior, are discussed in the next chapter.

Case 1.2: Virtue ethics
Consider stoicism and Aristotle's virtues and decide whether you would say any of the following individuals have good moral character: 1. Donald Trump 2. Joe Biden 3. Lindsey Lohan 4. Charlie Sheen 5. Michael Jackson 6. Britney Spears

Values

Values consist of what we prioritize in life; things that have importance, are desirable, or are worth something to us. Most people highly value family, friends, good health, honesty, safety, security, and respect, but not everyone will rank order these elements of value in the same way. How we prioritize can fluctuate given the situation we find ourselves in, as well. If I'm sick, then my health will come before all else and if I'm pushing a deadline at work then my career may come before other elements on my list. Relativists argue that no values are universally more important than others while universalists argue that some elements of value are more important than others like altruism.

According to Parsons (1967), **values** and shared culture are the basis for social systems that motivate us in terms of what we *should* do and determine our behavior in terms of what we *would* do. The idea is that our values to some degree drive our behaviors, however, just because someone values honesty doesn't mean that they are honest all the time. While I may be motivated to be honest, there can be situational factors where some other value comes into conflict – protecting my friend's feelings, for example. I may decide to lie regardless of how strongly I value honesty.

Case 1.3: Values
Everyone values the truth; however, we all lie at different times in our lives. Sometimes the truth isn't as valuable as protecting a relationship or avoiding emotional harm. Consider whether you would be willing to lie under any of the following circumstances and what competing values are at stake: 1. Your best friend is a drug dealer and doesn't want to be kicked out of college. They ask you to testify on their behalf at their student conduct hearing. 2. Another student broke into the online grading system and changed your grade from a "C" to an "A". 3. Someone you work with presented your work as their own. 4. You have access to top secret government documents that the general public should know about. 5. A friend applied to the company you work at and lied on their resume.

Duties and Obligations

Duties and **obligations** are usually terms that are used interchangeably. There is a distinction, however slight, among philosophers between the two terms. Generally, we have responsibilities to one another depending on our relationships with one another. To be considered a moral agent, we are expected to behave according to our responsibilities to one another. As a mother, I am expected to take care of my children – it is my special obligation because I have a special relationship with my children. If I do not behave according to this responsibility, then I'm shirking my moral responsibility and, in this example, there will also be legal consequences.

The distinction between **duties** and **obligations** often hinges on the relationship between the person who owes the duty and the person they owe the duty to (Jeske, 2021). **Duties** are considered by some philosophers as general duties we owe one another, like treating people with respect. These general duties are also sometimes referred to as natural duties and other times referred to as imperfect duties. **Supererogatories** are not required in the same way that duties and obligations are expected to be performed but are moral behavior that exceeds what is normally expected behavior. The most common example is a good Samaritan who intervenes at some personal risk to help someone that they don't owe a duty to.

Prima facie duties are acts where there is a significant relationship between the people involved in the moral dilemma at issue thus changing the nature of moral obligation that may exist between the parties involved. **Prima facie** means at first sight or on its face. It is a concept often used in the law to recognize special duties owed based on the relationship between parties involved in a dispute or legal thresholds that must be met in order to shift the burden of proof. For example, in discrimination cases, the plaintiff must make a **prima facie** case that they are in a protected class and that the person/agency discriminating treated them differently than others who are not in a protected class.

Within moral dilemmas, there are several types of **prima facie duties** which include:

Fidelity – explicit and implicit promises made between parties or agreements entered into that stem from previous actions between the parties
Reparation –a duty to make up for harms previously caused by others
Gratitude – a duty to repay others for past favors
Justice – prevent or correct mismatches between happiness and merit
Beneficence – improve conditions of others with respect to virtue, intelligence, or pleasure
Self-improvement – improve one's virtues or intelligence
Nonmaleficence – do not injure others (doing good for its own sake)

Duties and obligations are at the heart of deontological systems of ethics which we explore in the next chapter.

Case 1.4: Duties and obligations
You are in a lifeboat with four other people. You have enough food and water to last several weeks for the four of you. This will give you enough time to float into a shipping lane and be rescued. You will perish if the five of you consume all the food and water. There is a suggestion that one of you should die so the other four can live. Identify the duties/obligations that you owe one another and the values that are relevant to the decision. Consider whether the values and duties/obligations shift depending on any special relationships between the five passengers on the lifeboat.

Rational Choice Theory (RCT)

RCT is a theory that acknowledges we are all self-interested actors making decisions based on what benefits each of us the most. First recognized by Adam Smith in the 1700s, **RCT** is very similar to Ethical Egoism which is explored in the next chapter. **RCT** relies on a cost-benefit type analysis in decision-making. **RCT** has been explored by economists, social scientists, political scientists, and mathematicians. As an extension of **RCT**, Homans (1961) developed **Social Exchange**

Theory that applies cost-benefit analysis in personal and professional relationships. It is a system of exchange that determines the value of the relationship. Where the costs outweigh the benefits, then the relationship will suffer.

There are three issues that **RCT** struggles with explaining which include collective action, norms and obligations, and social structure. Collective action is altruistic behavior benefiting others more than it benefits the individual actor, which contradicts RCT. Following social norms and feeling a sense of obligation to others is also altruistic. And while RCT is a very individualistic theory, social structures are quite the opposite. Clearly RCT then can't explain all of our behaviors when making ethical decisions.

Case 1.5: Rational Choices
In a 2023 movie called *No Hard Feelings* a young woman, Maddie, is about to lose the home she grew up in. She can save her family home by taking a "job" dating a 19-year-old, Percy, as advertised by Percy's parents. Part of the assignment involves having sex with Percy while making sure that Percy doesn't discover the truth about their relationship. What should Maddie do? What if instead of taking this job, Maddie is using sex work to pay for her college education - does this change your opinion?

Moral/Ethical Dilemmas

We've all faced **moral/ethical dilemmas** where we are required to do one or more actions but can't so we must choose between the required actions. The choice, however, comes with a price – some type of potential harm that will occur because of the choice. There are a variety of types of dilemmas including epistemic, ontological, self-imposed, other-imposed, obligation-based, and prohibition-based. And there are many factors that impact how we resolve dilemmas like emotions, relationships to people involved in the resolution of the dilemma, the harm that can result, and the amount of time available to consider the choice.

Epistemic and ontological dilemmas involve conflicts between obligations and are very similar. If one is faced with a conflict of obligations and struggles to figure out which of the obligations has precedence over the other, then this is an **epistemic dilemma**. An example would be where a parent must choose between attending an event for one child over the other – one may take precedence over the other depending on the circumstances, but the parent will struggle none-the-less trying to determine which of the obligations they should attend. If there is no clear choice between obligations because neither of the obligations takes precedence over the other, then this is an **ontological dilemma**. An example is *Sophie's Choice* based on the movie with Meryl Streep (see Case 1.5). Sophie must ultimately decide which of her two children will live or die, a situation with no clear choice.

Self-imposed dilemmas happen because of one's own wrongdoing while **other-imposed dilemmas** happen because of another person's wrongdoing. If I double-book myself with two different engagements, then I've created my own dilemma. *Sophie's Choice* is an example of an **other-imposed dilemma** as Sophie is forced to choose between her children by a Nazi guard. An **obligation-based dilemma** is one where the possible choices are each obligatory (the example where I've double-booked myself) while a **prohibition-based dilemma** is one where all possible solutions are prohibited (*Sophie's Choice*).

Notice that these types of ethical dilemmas are not mutually exclusive. The *Sophie's Choice* dilemma is an ontological dilemma, other-imposed, and prohibition-based. And each dilemma can be resolved differently depending on many factors. For example, in *Sophie's Choice*, what impact does the age, gender, personality, and overall health of the child have on Sophie's decision? And with the Kobayashi Maru (Case 1.6 below), potential harm will play a big role in determining how a no-win scenario is resolved.

Case 1.6: Sophie's Choice
Sophie is the mother of two children sent to a Nazi concentration camp. One of the guards tells Sophie that she must choose which of her children will live or die and if she does not choose, then both will die. How can Sophie make this choice? What factors will she take into consideration? Age of the children? Gender? Relative health of each?

Case 1.7: Kobayashi Maru
This is a test administered to cadets in Star Fleet within the Star Trek universe. It is another name for a no-win scenario. It is a test to see how cadets handle intense situations where no matter what decisions they make, everything is lost. One cadet cheats and reprograms the test simulator so that they can beat the test and save everyone in the program. Is this fair? Would you be willing to cheat to avoid facing a no-win scenario? Have you faced a no-win scenario in your life? If so, how did you face this type of dilemma?

Case 1.8: The trolley-car dilemma
Perhaps the most famous moral dilemma is one where a trolley-car is barreling down the tracks about to hit five men who happen to be on the tracks. You are near a switch that will divert the trolley-car away from the five men, however, it will then be on a path towards a man sleeping on the other track. Would you divert the trolley-car? What factors impact your decision? Does it matter whether you know any of the men who might die? What if pushing someone in front of the trolley-car is the only way to divert it from hitting the five men who are on the tracks – would you be willing to push someone in front of the trolley-car to stop it?

Whistleblowing

Most people have seen someone cheat on a test or steal something from work. We can all identify with that feeling of knowing the right thing to do in those situations, but still not wanting to do it. Turning someone in for wrongdoing is a difficult decision even though it seems like a simple one. When someone decides to turn a coworker in for wrongdoing, this is known as **blowing the whistle** and the person turning in their coworker is known as a **whistleblower**. The term comes from police officers who used to blow whistles when they observed criminal behavior. **Whistleblowing** is:

> The disclosure by organization members (former or current) of illegal, immoral and illegitimate practices under the control of their employers to persons and organizations that may be able to effect action. (Near & Miceli, 1985, p. 4)

Types of wrongdoing in the workplace include stealing, waste, mismanagement, safety problems, sexual harassment, unfair discrimination, and legal violations (Near et al., 2004). People who blow the whistle on wrongful conduct within an organization do so for altruistic reasons typically, but whistleblowers can also be motived to earn some type of reward offered by the organization for turning in stealing, for example.

Whistleblowers are not disgruntled employees. According to Brewer and Selden (1998), they rank among the most productive, valued, and committed members of their organizations. **Whistleblowers** are normal people who have a strong conscience, are highly committed to the formal goals of their organization, and they have a strong sense of professional responsibility. **Whistleblowers** are less motivated by job security and more motivated by regard for the public interest. They report high levels of job commitment and job satisfaction (Brewer & Selden 1998).

Unfortunately, **whistleblowers** can face negative consequences for turning someone in formally or informally. Under the Whistleblower Protection Act (1989), The Sarbanes-Oxley Act (2002), as well as many state laws, **whistleblowers** are generally protected from retaliation. Many famous examples exist of **whistleblowers** who were not treated well, despite the many legal protections that exist. The existence of unions is a direct result of the many workplace safety issues and poor working conditions found within manufacturing, as well as unethically low pay for workers, and while unions generally protect **whistleblowers**, they are not always successful in doing so. Within the justice system, there are several high-profile instances of **whistleblowing** (see Cases 1.9 and 1.10 below).

Case 1.9: NSA and classified documents
Edward Snowden was a former employee of the National Security Agency (NSA) who claimed to notify his superiors and other employees about the unethical misuse of private information collected unnecessarily from U.S. citizens. Out of frustration, Snowden leaked highly classified information in 2013 regarding surveillance programs the NSA operated. He eventually fled to Russia to avoid espionage charges and theft of government property. What would you do if you were in Snowden's shoes? Would you leak highly classified government documents?

Case 1.10: Fair Game
In 2003, President Bush famously declared in his State of the Union address that Sadam Hussein was trying to acquire Uranium from Africa to bolster Iraq's nuclear weapons program. In response, Joe Wilson, a former U.S. Diplomat, wrote an opinion piece in the New York Times disputing President's Bush's claim. One week later, Wilson's wife, Valerie Plame, was outed as an undercover CIA agent, having her identity leaked illegally to the press by several members of the Bush administration. Plame had to be released from the CIA after having her identity released and her operations were shut down, placing many people at risk of great harm. The movie *Fair Game* depicts the events that led up to Plame ultimately testifying before Congress regarding her identity being illegally leaked. Should Wilson have challenged the President? Was Plame's identity leak retaliation?

Collecting Data

When social scientists collect data, whether it's quantitative or qualitative, they must follow some rules to prevent harm to the subjects of their study. This is why every research study usually begins with going through a review process by an independent body known as an

Institutional Review Board (IRB). The **IRB** will ensure that the researchers comply with protecting the research subjects. Researchers must submit to their **IRB** an explanation in detail of what data they plan on collecting, how long they plan on collecting the data, and how they will collect the data. IRBs typically have an expedited process for reviewing research plans that are low risk to their subjects (e.g. simply reviewing existing data that has already been collected through a survey). Where there are special populations that are particularly vulnerable, like juveniles and individuals who are under correctional control, extra review is necessary and can often require an informal or possibly a formal hearing with the **IRB** to ensure proper controls are in place to protect the research subjects.

Social science research requires protecting the identity of the research subjects by promising anonymity where possible. This is easy to promise where surveys are collected without identifying information from the research subjects. If it is not possible to collect data anonymously, then the researchers must promise confidentiality with respect to the research subjects' identifiable information which is possible by not connecting the test subject's identifiable information to their responses. Research subjects should also be made aware of their ability to refuse to be part of the research study at any time during the process of collecting the data. All these protections of identity, confidentiality, and voluntariness are articulated to research subjects either in writing or orally which is known as informed consent.

Even with all these protections for research subjects, some ethical issues still arise with the collection of data specific to the field of criminal justice. For example, it is nearly impossible to have a randomized experimental design when conducting tests in the field. In a randomized experimental design, the researcher can choose which subjects are in a control group that don't receive an intervention being tested. For example, if I want to test to see whether diversion courts are effective, I can't as a researcher decide which subjects will be placed into the diversion courts and which will not. Only a judge can make those types of decisions. Studying police officers can also be challenging as their jobs are very dangerous making it difficult to collect observational data that places the researcher in precarious circumstances. These are the types of dilemmas that come from studying subjects in the real world as opposed to within the confines of laboratory setting where the environment is easily controlled.

Other moral dilemmas arise simply because of the nature of crime and victimization itself. Studying crime focuses on illegal behavior which can be difficult to observe. Social scientists in the criminal justice field often rely on self-report data from those who are committing illegal acts, victims of crime, and bystanders who will be affected by the trauma of the criminal event itself. Crime is very traumatic for victims, perpetrators of crime, and even bystanders. Crafting questions that avoid causing further trauma becomes rather tricky in these circumstances as a result. Finding research subjects who are willing to talk about their traumatic experiences within the criminal justice system can be difficult, as well. And getting agencies to allow access to research subjects is difficult since most agencies do not want bad publicity from a research study that exposes problems within the system.

Case 1.11: Taser study
Todak et al. (2018) conducted a study to test the impact that tasers have on cognitive ability. They began their research with 21 new recruit police officers who are exposed to tasers during their training. The researchers tested cognitive functioning prior to taser exposure and then at several intervals after the taser exposure. What ethical issues do you see researchers facing with the collection of this type of research with respect to the effects of tasers on the human body? What problems do you suppose the researchers might have encountered when collecting this data? How can the researchers overcome these obstacles?

Conclusion

What would you do if presented with a wish as the three brothers were given from the Harry Potter parable? Would you wish for world peace?

A cure for cancer? Even the third brother who fares better than his siblings, wishes for a cloak of invisibility so that he can hide from death. His only saving grace is that he eventually sheds the cloak after living a long and fruitful life, passing it along to his son. The three brothers themselves were powerful wizards so presumably they could conjure up quite a lot for themselves as it stands. So, while the third brother didn't succumb to the same vices as his siblings, he still wished for something that is rather selfish.

While this chapter explores what morality is, how we study morality, what we value, whether we owe one another any duties, and what our obligations are to society, the next chapter looks at systems of ethics. We now have the foundation necessary to apply these ethical systems to a variety of moral/ethical dilemmas. The systems of ethics we explore next will focus both on duties one owes, as well as the consequences of our behavior.

Debate Topics for In-Class Discussion

1. Raising the minimum wage
    a. *Pro* – giving earners a living wage; increases taxes collected by the government which benefits society overall
    b. *Con* – hurts small business owners; costs are passed onto the consumer
2. Forcing homeless to be hospitalized for mental health
    a. *Pro* – provides mental health care for individuals who may not be capable of helping themselves; gets people off the streets which is a dangerous place to live
    b. *Con* – violates individual rights of autonomy; may overburden the mental health care system

Terms

Morality
Moral Relativism
Ethics
Meta-ethics
Professional ethics
Applied ethics
Normative ethics
Situational ethics
Virtue ethics
Virtues
Values
Duties
Obligations
Supererogatories
Prima facie duties
Rational Choice Theory (RCT)
Social Exchange Theory
Moral/ethical dilemmas
Epistemic dilemma
Ontological dilemma
Self-imposed dilemmas
Other-imposed dilemmas
Obligation-based dilemmas
Prohibition-based dilemmas
Whistleblowing
Whistleblower
Institutional Review Board

References

Brewer, G. A., & Selden, S. C. (1998). Whistle blowers in the federal civil service: New evidence of the public service ethic. *Journal of public administration research and theory, 8*(3), 413-440.

Gert, B. & Gert, J. (2020). The Definition of Morality. *The Stanford Encyclopedia of Philosophy.*

Homans, G. (1961). *Social Behavior: Its Elementary Forms.* New York: Harcourt Brace Jovanovich.

Jeske, D. (2021). Special Obligations. *The Stanford Encyclopedia of Philosophy.*

Kagan, S. (2018). *Normative ethics*. Routledge.

Near, J. & Miceli, M. (1985). Organizational Dissidence: The Case of Whistleblowing. *Journal of Business Ethics,* 4(1), 1-16.

Near, J. P., Rehg, M. T., Van Scotter, J. R., & Miceli, M. P. (2004). Does type of wrongdoing affect the whistle-blowing process?. *Business Ethics Quarterly,* 14(2), 219-242.

Parsons, T. (1967). *Sociological Theory and Modern Society*. Glencoe, Ill.: Free Press.

Sarbanes-Oxley Act of 2002, Public Law 107-204, Statutes at Large 116 (2002): 745-810.

Todak, N., White, M. D., Dario, L. M., & Borrego, A. R. (2018). Overcoming the challenges of experimental research: Lessons from a criminal justice case study involving TASER exposure. *Evaluation Review,* 42(3), 358-385.

Whistleblower Protection Act of 1989, Public Law 12, U.S. Statutes at Large 103 (1989): 16-35.

Chapter 2
Systems of Ethics

Chapter Objectives

1. Identify various systems of ethics and whether they are deontological or teleological.
2. Apply each of the systems of ethics to a variety of ethical dilemmas.
3. Demonstrate an understanding of how ethical systems impact our daily lives, as well as society.

Introduction

In the last episode of the final season of Black Mirror, a demon comes to earth and mentors a young woman. She has been commanded to kill three people in three days or Armageddon will be unleashed destroying all of civilization. What will she decide to do? If she kills only bad people, does that make her behavior seem more acceptable? By what guidelines do we observe her behavior and determine whether it is moral? Ethical systems consist of sets of principles that define what is moral so depending on which ethical system one subscribes to, then we can judge whether her decisions are moral or not.

In the last chapter, we explored two theories of human behavior – rational choice and social exchange - that are not considered ethical systems but impact our perceptions of what is socially considered to be good and bad conduct. Now we turn our attention to ethical systems that guide behavior and give us a way to judge whether an action is moral or not. Ethical systems are prescriptive in terms of giving us the principles that should guide our behaviour. They are also authoritative and considered valid mechanisms for judging behavior. Ethical systems are logically impartial or universal and not self-serving. Within normative ethics, there are two primary types of systems of ethics which include systems that focus on behavior and systems that focus on character. Virtue ethics and natural law focus on character while the remaining systems focus on behavior. Within behavioral ethical systems, there are two ways to consider behavior – either the consequences of our actions or the duties we owe to one another.

Deontological systems are duty-based ethical systems where ethical behavior is determined based on duties or obligations within relationships among individuals and groups. In a deontological system, the important determinant for judging whether an act is moral is the motive or intent of the actor. **Deontological** systems include **Kantian** ethics or **Ethical Formalism** and religious ethics or **Modified Divine Command Theory**. **Teleological** systems, on the other hand, are considered consequentialist ethics because ethical behavior is determined based on the outcome or consequences of the behavior or action. **Utilitarianism** and **Ethical Egoism** are both **teleological** systems of ethics. We will first consider religion, natural law, and positivism as these are considered some of the first ethical systems.

Religion

It is debated amongst scholars whether religious moral reasoning takes precedence over philosophical moral reasoning. **Religion** is an ethical system focusing on duties we owe in terms of following the word of God and is considered the basis for moral reasoning beginning with Christianity, Judaism, and Islam. All three religions believe in only one God (monotheistic) and consider Abraham as a central figure within each of their religious texts – the bible, the Torah, and the Qur'an, respectively. **Modified Divine Command Theory (MDCT)** posits that God is a loving God who loves each of us equally and anything that conflicts with what God wills/commands is considered immoral (Adams, 1987). There are many criticisms of MDCT including:

1. How do we know God is good- what is the basis for believing that God is good?

2. An omnipotent God who can do anything but is simultaneously incapable of doing harm is contradictory.
3. If whatever God commands one to do is therefore a moral act, then God must command himself to engage in moral behavior which seems incongruous.
4. If God commands us to engage in moral behavior, then we have no autonomy.
5. With so many sects and/or denominations of religions, how do we know which one to follow – which of these is the true command of God?

Case 2.1: Religion
Global trends of religious affiliation constantly fluctuate. Christians are declining in the United States but will remain the larges religious sect worldwide over the next 30 years. Muslims will increase in numbers almost equaling the number of Christians. Atheists will decline worldwide despite seeing increases in the United States and France (Hackett et al., 2012). What impact do these fluctuations have on societies and their interactions with one another globally? How do you feel about the state of religious affiliation over the next three decades?

There are many different religious sects, however, most organized religions express some version of The Golden Rule. Over 16% of the world's population does not affiliate with any organized religion which is essentially equal in numbers to Catholics worldwide (Hackett, 2012). While many are atheists – believing there is no God - many of the unaffiliated ascribe to some type of spirituality. Religious affiliations we will highlight include (in order of popularity): Christianity, Islam, Hinduism, Buddhism, Judaism, and Confucianism.

Christianity

Christians, followers of the teachings of Jesus who is proclaimed to be the son of God, make up almost a third of the world's population (Hackett et al., 2012). The largest denomination of Christianity is the Catholic Church making up more than half of Christians globally

(Britannica[b], 2023). The **Christian** faith follows the teachings of Jesus who was born a Jew, poor, and a member of an oppressed minority class, conquered and controlled by the Romans. The bible is the holy word of God, written by a variety of sources. What does it mean to be a Christian?

> The masses of men live with their backs constantly against the wall. They are the poor, the disinherited, the dispossessed. What does our religion say to them? The issue is not what it counsels them to do for others whose need may be greater, but what religion offers to meet their own needs. (Thurman, 1976, p. 3)

Thurman's interpretation of Jesus' teachings shows clear parallels to modern day oppression through slavery and Jim Crow laws. Thurman's book inspired Dr. Martin Luther King, Jr. prior to the Montgomery bus boycott.

But where did Jesus find his inspiration? Most likely from Judaism, as well as from stories told by prophets and other visionaries of the time, both Greek and Roman, Jewish, and Gentile (Levine, 2006). While it's impossible to know details, there is some agreement regarding Jesus' life:

> Most scholars agree that Jesus was baptized by John, debated with fellow Jews on how best to live according to God's will, engaged in healings and exorcisms, taught in parables, gathered male and female followers in Galilee, went to Jerusalem, and was crucified by Roman soldiers during the governorship of Pontius Pilate (26-36 CE). (Levine, 2006, p. 4)

The Golden Rule: In everything, do to others as you would have them do to you; for this is the law and the prophets (Jesus, Matthew 7:12).

Case 2.2: Christianity
In a 2023 U.S. Supreme Court case, a website designer refused to create a website for a same-sex marriage couple citing a conflict of the designers' Christian faith. The Court sided with the web designer citing First Amendment protections for all individuals working in businesses where they might feel their values are compromised when creating expressive content. According to the justices who dissented, this decision "grants a business open to the public a constitutional right to refuse to serve members of a protected class" (*303 Creative LLC v. Elenis*, 2023). Do you feel that the Court made the correct moral decision? Why or why not?

Islam

Muslims, followers of Allah and the prophet Mohammed, make up almost a quarter of the world's population (Hackett et al., 2012). There are Five Pillars that all Muslims are duty-bound to obey, and they include a profession of faith, praying five times daily, paying alms or a tax used to help the poor, fasting during Ramadan, and making a pilgrimage to Mecca if possible. The Qur'an is the holy word of God. Sharia, Islamic law, governs society so there is no real separation of church and state. The **Islamic** faith is rooted in Iman which consists of six articles of their faith (Britannica[a], 2023):

1. God
2. Angels
3. Revelation (Qur'an)
4. Prophets (Adam, Noah, Abraham, Moses, Jesus, and Mohammed)
5. Day of Resurrection (akin to Judgement Day)
6. Divine Decree (everything comes from Allah, both good and bad)

The Golden Rule: Not one of you truly believes until you wish for others what you wish for yourself (The Prophet Mohammed, Hadith).

Case 2.3: Islamaphobia
Since the 9/11 terrorist attacks, the U.S. government has explored many options to ensure the safety of its citizens against future terrorist attacks including Congress passing the "See Something, Say Something Act" (the "Act"), an amendment to the Homeland Security Act of 2002. The Act encourages ordinary citizens to suspect and report someone based on perceived demeanor and/or overall appearance without the usual requirement of articulable suspicion under *Terry v. Ohio* (1968). Hate crimes in the U.S. spiked dramatically in 2001 post 9/11 from under 30 per year on average to around 480 reported incidents with over 550 victims. Do you think the See Something, Say Something Act encourages potential discrimination against Muslims? Why or why not?

Hinduism

Approximately 15% of the world's population practices **Hinduism** and Hindus primarily come from India and Nepal (Hackett et al., 2012). Hinduism does not come from a single source, nor is it founded by a singular prophet, and it lacks any centralized organizational structure or authority. There is also no one sacred text, although many consider the Veda their sacred text. As such, the Hindu faith varies greatly. In some Hindu philosophies, there are various rituals that are necessary for salvation, some believe there is a creator who has the power to destroy the universe, and some believe in Karma through reincarnation. Hindus believe they have duties related to one's social position (caste system) and stage of life and this concept is known as dharma.

> One striking feature of Hinduism is that practice takes precedence over belief. What a Hindu does is more important than what a Hindu believes. Hinduism is not credal. Adherence to dharma is therefore not an acceptance of certain beliefs, but the practice or performance of certain duties, which are defined in accordance with dharmic social stratification. (Flood, 1996, p. 12)

The Golden Rule: This is the sum of duty: do not do to others what would cause pain if done to you (Mahabharata 5:1317).

Case 2.4: Hinduism
A part of the Hindu religion is based on a caste system which has been a part of Indian culture, religion, and politics for thousands of years. Caste systems define your position withing society based on education, occupation, and family ties. But caste systems can be rigid and discriminatory. Since the 1950s, legal and social changes have begun to occur in India. What impact will these changes have on the Hindu religion? Do we have a caste system in the United States with respect to social position based on education, occupation, and family ties?

Buddhism

About 7% of the world's population practices **Buddhism** as it is both a religion and a philosophy steeped in spiritualism (Hackett et al., 2012). Its central figure, the Blessed Budha, was born in India and is not a name so much as a title. Buddhism eventually spread across Asia and has some striking similarities to Hinduism. Budha is said to have achieved enlightenment and continually reincarnates after spending some time in heaven. Buddhism values "the cultivation of the ten 'perfections': generosity, morality, desirelessness, vigour, wisdom, patience, truthfulness, resolve, loving kindness, and equanimity" (Gethin, 1998, p. 18).

The Golden Rule: Treat not others in ways that you yourself would find hurtful (Udana-Varga 5.18).

Judaism

There are approximately 0.2% of Jewish people around the world, almost half of whom live in Israel (Hackett et al., 2012). **Judaism** is older than any other religion, relying on the Torah and Talmud for guidance. Abraham and Jesus are recognized as profits, but Jesus is not considered the son of God. **Judaism** requires daily prayer, reading frequently from the Torah, observing the Sabbath every week, as well as some dietary restrictions. Historically, the Jews have been villainized by Christians for rejecting Jesus as the son of God:

> The Jews were a 'special people,' 'the chosen people,' as it says in the Bible, chosen by God to be the vehicle of his revelation. But they had rejected Jesus, and therefore were accursed and condemned to lowly status until, in the fullness of time, they would recognize Jesus. (Solomon, 2009, p. 2)

The Golden Rule: What is hateful to you do not do to your neighbour. This is the whole Torah; all the rest is commentary (Hillel, Talmud, Shabbat 31a).

Confucianism

Confucianism is "a tradition open to religious values" and considered an eastern religion and philosophy that is as much a way of life as it is a part of the political establishment (Yao, 2000, p. 11). It was established as a new philosophy by Confucius (551 – 479 BCE) and his followers. **Confucianism** is considered a humanistic philosophy that values family and social harmony (Juergensmeyer, 2005). The Four Books and the Five Classics, written after Confucius' death, espouse how one should live one's life in the pursuit of learning and attainment of perfect virtue.

The Golden Rule: One word which sums up the basis of all good conduct . . . loving kindness. Do not do to others what you do not want done to yourself (Confucius, Analects 15.23).

Natural Law and Positivism

Natural Law is the idea that principles of morals and rights are inherent in nature and not human-made. Such laws are discovered by reason but exist apart from humankind. Aristotle and Thomas Aquinas are largely considered to be the forefathers of natural law. The focus is on human beings as rational actors, able to rely on reasoning in decision-making. According to natural law:

> . . . any sane person is capable of seeing that life, knowledge, fellowship, offspring, and a few other such basic aspects of

> human existence are, as such, good, i.e. worth having . . . (Finnis, 2011, p. 30)

According to **Natural Law**, humans pursue these goods, these things worth having, and their pursuit of these things is both universal and morally right. It is a teleological system of ethics focusing on virtue. Some argue that it is also deontological in terms of creating duties that protect human rights.

Positivism, a type of legal reasoning, was created to supplement **Natural Law** theory and focuses primarily on human rights, peace, and contracts. As such, **Positivism** is more deontological than **Natural Law**. Thomas Hobbes contributed to the development of legal positivism which was later expanded upon by Jeremy Bentham. While Natural Law exists inherently in nature, legal positivism is codified and shaped by humans. Examples of the influence of natural law and positivism can be found in the Declaration of Independence for the United States and the Universal Declaration of Human Rights of the United Nations.

Case 2.5: Natural Law
According to Finnis (2011), there are seven basic goods that are self-evident including life, knowledge, play, aesthetic experience, sociability, practical reasonableness, and religion. Do you agree that there are seven basic goods that are self-evident that people strive towards universally? Do you believe those seven goods remain constant over time, across cultures, and gender norms? What would you add and/or subtract from this list of basic goods?

Utilitarianism (teleological)

Jeremy Bentham (1748 – 1832) and John Stuart Mill (1806 – 1873) were major proponents of **Utilitarianism**, believing that the morality of an action should be determined by how much it contributes to the good of the majority. "The needs of the many outweigh the needs of the few or the one" was famously uttered by Spock on Star Trek when he sacrificed his life to save an entire ship of crewmates. Another example is the famous trolley-car dilemma mentioned in the last chapter. Killing one person seems on the surface to be better than killing five, but when we start to explore the finer details, then the answers get a bit murkier.

There are two types of **Utilitarianism** – Act and Rule. With **Act Utilitarianism**, an action is examined to determine its utility. This is the simplest of the two types of **Utilitarianism** as it requires little deliberation. **Act Utilitarianism** is best exemplified in the trolley-car dilemma. Killing one person is preferable to killing five people so under **Act Utilitarianism**, the decision becomes obvious.

With **Rule Utilitarianism**, one judges an action and the consequences of that action with respect to any precedent it might set and any long-term utility because of that action. In the trolley-car dilemma, perhaps not interfering with the trolley-car is the answer because then you are playing God, intervening, and valuing the five lives over the one. What if the one person you're saving turns out to be the next Hitler? What if the five people you're are condemning to death will someday save the planet?

Rule Utilitarianism may be closer to the principles of **Ethical Formalism** because both ethical systems consider general, universal laws. The difference between Rule Utilitarianism and Ethical Formalism is that **Rule Utilitarianism** takes into consideration long-term consequences of the act in question. Meanwhile, under **Ethical Formalism** the rules themselves are judged right or wrong depending on the motives behind them.

Some critiques of **Utilitarianism** point out that there is a problem with trying to measure pleasures and benefits which are not of equal value. In the trolley-car dilemma, for example, how do we measure the lives of the six people who could potentially be killed? Who decides their value? Quantifying all the possible components is challenging not only with **Utilitarianism**, but with any cost-benefit analysis.

Utilitarianism also presumes that while deciding and weighing the potential consequences of all possible actions, we can predict all possible outcomes based on those actions. With the trolley-car dilemma, how do we know that changing the track for the trolley will kill anyone? The changing of the track, the fact that there are multiple people on the track, the time of day, the length of track are all factors that could easily change the possible outcomes. Until a decision is made in any ethical dilemma there's really no way of knowing what will happen.

And there is little concern for individual rights within **Utilitarianism**. As a practical matter, taking individual rights into consideration then adds yet another layer of measuring value and human worth that is challenging in a cost-benefit analysis. In the Star Trek example, Spock sacrifices himself, but there are many examples where soldiers are sent into battle and death is almost certain. Their sacrifice is considered what's best for the needs of the many civilians they are sworn to protect, overriding any individual rights of the soldier.

Case 2.6: Utilitarianism
In *Waking Ned Devine*, a man, Ned Devine, wins the lottery and dies of a heart attack. He has no living relatives that could inherit his new fortune, almost 7 million Irish pounds. Imagine that you discover your friend Ned who has just died of a heart attack with the winning lottery ticket in his hand. What would you take into consideration before deciding what to do with the lottery ticket? Would you pretend to be Ned and claim the winnings? What if Ned had claimed the winnings and they are sitting in a suitcase in his house – would you be willing to take the cash as opposed to a lottery ticket? Would you share any of the winnings with the people who live in your small community of 52 residents? What if you found out Ned had a distant relative who he hated and never spoke to? If you apply Act Utilitarian and then Rule Utilitarian principles, what decisions do you come to?

Ethics of Care (teleological)

Carol Gilligan (1993) is considered the first to identify an **Ethic of Care**. It focuses on relationships rather than the individual and posits that balancing concern for oneself and for others is a marker for moral maturity (Gilligan, 1993). The **Ethics of Care** has been characterized as a feminist approach, focusing on attributes commonly valued by women. Tronto (1989) expands on the **Ethics of Care** by identifying several aspects of the moral dimension of care. First, the caregiver must be attentive to learn the needs of the person they are caring for which requires a lot of time and patience. Second, the nature of the caregiver/cared-for relationship is one where the cared-for is dependent upon the caregiver. This leaves the cared-for vulnerable and gives a lot of power to the caregiver. Finally, there are problems that arise when considering the particulars of caring for someone and meeting their individual needs.

While **Ethics of Care** centers on relationships and the duties owed with respect to caregiving, the moral dimension of care is focused on the actions of the caregiver making it a teleological system of ethics. There are two different kinds of caring – things we care about and people that we care for. For example, I am a college professor who cares deeply *about* learning. And, in my profession, I spend most of my time *caring for* my students. Caring is essentially a commitment to something or someone who is the object of the caring.

Case 2.7: Ethics of Care
In *The Southern Book Club's Guide to Slaying Vampires,* Patricia must decide whether to care for her aging mother-in-law, Mary, who has dementia. Patricia's husband works long hours, and she is a stay-at-home mother of two teenage children. Mary can be difficult to care for as she will say horrible things sometimes, get confused easily, and can wander off at any time. Your husband has two siblings who refuse to take Mary in simply because it's too much work. What would you do if you were Patricia? Do you take Mary in and care for her? Why or why not? If so, how would you approach caring for Mary?

Ethical Egoism (teleological)

Ethical Egoism can be broken down into two areas that include **Egoism** and **Psychological Egoism**. **Ethical Egoism** defines the pursuit of self-interest as a moral good in how we ought to act. It is the pursuit of what is in our own best interests, however, it does not exclude acting in the interests of others particularly where long-term we expect to receive help in return. **Psychological Egoism** posits that humans seek self-interest and that we do so because it is what comes natural to each of us. **Psychological Egoism** highlights not how we ought to act, but how we do act.

There are three primary arguments that support **Ethical Egoism** as a system guiding ethical behavior. First, we each know intimately our own wants and needs much better than the needs and wants of others. Pursuing our own wants and needs is far superior to overseeing the wants and needs of others or having someone oversee our own wants and needs. Of course, there are exceptions with children or anyone who is unable to care for themselves. Second, valuing our own wants and needs is important because it places value on the individual rather than placing value on others over the individual as is the case with altruism. And finally, there are fundamental principles that if we adhere to them then it is in our own best interests (Rachels, 2003). According to Hobbes, if we don't follow the Golden Rule ourselves, then we will suffer the consequences of being treated disrespectfully in return.

There are several arguments against **Ethical Egoism** being a system that guides moral behavior. The strongest argument is that it places a greater importance on the self over all others. Placing one group of people as more important over the needs and interests of other groups is a type of discrimination that can lead to arbitrariness and bad outcomes in terms of guiding moral behavior. And yet in most moral decisions, we place the highest value on the impact our decision will have on our own personal interests.

Case 2.8: Ethical Egoism
The Central Park Five, who were all later exonerated, is an example of a dilemma commonly faced in the justice system. A group of teenagers were detained and interrogated by police regarding the rape and beating of a jogger in Central Park during the spring of 1989. Each of the teenagers was coerced into admitting being present during the rape being promised leniency if they cooperated. If you were faced with telling the truth and facing stiff potential penalties in court versus lying and accepting a plea agreement, which would be in your best interest? What if you must implicate someone else to accept a plea agreement? How do you determine what is in your best interest? What impact does the harm you might cause others involved in the case have on your decision?

Ethical Formalism (deontological)

Now we switch focus to duty-based or deontological systems. We've already explored one deontological system, religion, which focuses on our duty to follow God's commands. **Ethical Formalism**, according to **Immanuel Kant** (1724–1804), posits that the only act or intent that is intrinsically good is one that comes from a good will. The consequences of an act are irrelevant while the intent of the actor is everything.

Kant believed that our personal, moral worth is dependent upon doing one's duty. **Kant** believed in **hypothetical imperatives** and **categorical imperatives** that govern moral behavior. A **hypothetical imperative** is an if/then statement where an act is necessary to achieve an end goal. If I study diligently, then I will earn a good grade on my test. **Categorical imperatives** by contrast do not require an act to achieve the end goal. Instead, they are actions that require no further justification or rationalization and are guiding principles for moral behavior. Conforming to the categorical imperative is necessary to be good.

There are three basic tenets associated with **Kant's categorical imperative**. The first requires the actor to treat their moral decisions as if they apply to everyone as universal laws. This means that if it's acceptable for me to lie in a situation, then it is acceptable for everyone to lie in that situation. **Kant** also believed that we shouldn't use one another as a means to an end. This means that if I volunteer to help people, then I shouldn't be doing this just to enhance my resume and impress future employers. And the final tenet **Kant** espoused requires that we engage in moral acts of our own free will without having to be coerced into engaging in moral behavior. These three tenets constitute **Kant's categorical imperative**.

Ethical Formalism is an absolutist system where if something is wrong, it is wrong all the time like murder or lying. **Kant** believed, however, that if you're being attacked and the attacker doesn't deserve the truth, then so long as you don't intend to deceive you could potentially lie and it would be moral. As a result, **Ethical Formalism** is unresponsive to extreme circumstances where murder and lying may be justified under other ethical systems. Also, morality is limited to duties, however, problems arise when there are conflicting duties. Finally, having good intentions doesn't necessarily lead to positive consequences so prioritizing intent over outcomes is not always optimal.

Case 2.9: Ethical Formalism
A common ethical dilemma that all employers face is what to do with employees who aren't a good fit in your agency. Maybe it's someone who complains all the time or someone who does the minimum to get by. Some people, even after discussing their behavior, will persist in undesirable behavior because it's engrained in their personality. Do you push this individual to the point where they will want to leave? And if they do decide to leave, will you be a reference for them? Apply the ethical systems we've discussed so far in this chapter – do you have different results based on the system you apply?

Conclusion

Most people rely on a combination of the ethical systems discussed in this chapter when coming to a moral decision. This method of combining ethical systems into one overall perspective of morality is called common-sense morality (Adler, 1970). This approach to ethical decision-making has some advantages like not getting caught up in the rigidity of prescribed rules while being able to focus on both duties and outcomes. It's like moral relativism discussed in the previous chapter, however, with one important difference. Moral relativism is entirely subjective and no one viewpoint is considered superior to another. However, with common-sense morality the moral principle of an ethical system is considered in conjunction with how others resolve moral dilemmas.

If you've been reading this chapter thinking how it would be impossible to choose one ethical system over another when making a moral decision, then common-sense morality explains why. You probably even recognized times when you subscribed to one or another of these systems, as well as times when you combined several. In the next chapter we will look at the moral reasoning process, fallacies of moral reasoning, and the stages of moral development.

Debate Topics for In-Class Discussion

1. Eliminate the use of confessions in police investigations
    a. *Pro* – eliminates possibility of illegally obtaining a confession and violating human rights
    b. *Con* – hurts solving cases as confessions are commonly used
2. Eliminate cash bail
    a. *Pro* – takes a huge burden off the jails and reduces the overreliance on cash bail which is discriminatorily applied disproportionately to people of color
    b. *Con* – allows some defendants to continue committing crimes without being incapacitated long enough to control their behavior

Terms

Deontological
Teleological
Religion
Modified Divine Command Theory (MDCT)
Christian
Christianity
Muslim
Islamic
Hinduism
Buddhism
Judaism
Confucianism
Natural Law
Positivism
Utilitarianism
Act Utilitarianism
Rule Utilitarianism
Ethics of Care
Ethical Egoism
Egoism
Psychological Egoism
Ethical Formalism
Immanuel Kant
Hypothetical imperatives
Categorical imperatives

References

303 Creative LLC v. Elenis, 600 U.S. _____ (2023).

Adams, R. M. (1987). The virtue of faith and other essays in philosophical theology. Oxford University Press.

Adler, M. J. (1970). The time of our lives: The ethics of common sense.

Britannica[a], T. Editors of Encyclopaedia (June, 2023). *Pillars of Islam. Encyclopedia Britannica.* https://www.britannica.com/topic/Pillars-of-Islam

Britannica[b], T. Editors of Encyclopaedia (June, 2023). *Roman Catholicism summary. Encyclopedia Britannica.* https://www.britannica.com/summary/Roman-Catholicism

Finnis, J. (2011). *Natural law and natural rights.* Oxford University Press.

Flood, G. D. (1996). *An introduction to Hinduism.* Cambridge University Press.

Gethin, R. (1998). *The foundations of Buddhism.* OUP Oxford.

Gilligan, C. (1993). *In a different voice: Psychological theory and women's development.* Harvard university press.

Hackett, C., Grim, B., Stonawski, M., Skirbekk, V., Potančoková, M., & Abel, G. (2012). The global religious landscape. *Washington, DC: Pew Research Center.*

Juergensmeyer, M. (Ed.). (2005). *Religion in global civil society.* Oxford University Press.

Levine, A. J. (2006). *The historical Jesus in context.* Princeton University Press.

Rachels, J. (2003). "Ethical Egoism," *The Elements of Moral Philosophy,* 4th ed. McGraw-Hill.

Solomon, N. (2009). *Judaism.* Sterling Publishing Company, Inc.

Terry v. Ohio, 392 U.S. 1 (1968).

Thurman, H. (1976). *Jesus and the Disinherited.* Beacon Press.

Tronto, J. (1989). Women and caring: What can feminists learn about morality from caring. *Gender/body/knowledge: Feminist reconstructions of being and knowing*, 172-187.

Yao, X. (2000). *An introduction to Confucianism*. Cambridge University Press.

Chapter 3
Moral Reasoning

Chapter Objectives

1. Understand the process of moral reasoning.
2. Identify the moral facts and/or issues within a moral dilemma.
3. Recognize fallacies in moral reasoning.
4. Think critically when resolving conflicting obligations.
5. Explore ethical issues within the context of deviant and delinquent behavior.

Introduction

During the COVID-19 pandemic, we each faced ethical decisions like whether you should wear a mask, go out in public, and eventually whether you should get a vaccine. So many factors affected these decisions and many people died because of their decisions. Up until this point, we've been considering moral dilemmas and how to resolve them without considering the process we should go through to resolve those dilemmas. Ethical decision-making requires humans to go through a process of moral reasoning. The process itself is as important as the final decision. With the pandemic, where people got their facts from, and the reliability of that information had a huge impact on their decisions.

Moral philosophers like Socrates believed that we go through this process by discussing the dilemma and all its dimensions. It is how the **Socratic method** was established – finding answers to thorny questions through a process of questions and answers. The **Socratic method** is still widely used in law classrooms as an instrument to learn legal theory and precedents. Now we turn our attention to the process of moral reasoning. As with most processes there are some hidden traps which we explore by identifying the various fallacies in argumentation. There are also several theories regarding our moral development which begins at a very early age. This chapter also discusses deviant behavior and delinquency.

Moral Reasoning

The **moral reasoning** process is as much about how we should behave as why we should behave in certain ways. It is a process that involves identifying the moral facts and/or issues, sorting out all the moral considerations, resolving the conflicts between duties and/or obligations, accepting that you may need to change your mind, being able to articulate a reason for your decision, and learning from the experience. According to Hume (1739), a moral judgment is more than just the facts, it involves a general moral principle, as well. This is known as **Hume's Law**. Hume (1739) also argued that emotions play a critical role in moral reasoning.

The **moral reasoning** process is a decision-making type of process. An economic approach to decision-making commonly used in government agencies is a **cost-benefit analysis**. In the last chapter, I mentioned **cost-benefit analysis**, which is one approach to general decision-making. It is sometimes also used in moral decision-making. This approach requires placing an economic value on each of the tangible costs and benefits like how much the labor will cost to provide security in airports. As mentioned in the last chapter, however, quantifying non-tangible costs can be tricky and gets lost in a traditional cost-benefit analysis. In the airport security example, one of the costs of not hiring enough security or not having adequate security (well-trained, professional agents) is that a terrorist causes the kind of costs we saw as a result of 9/11. How do you quantify the loss of thousands of lives, the impact on their families, and the ensuing economic crisis?

Moral philosophers like Socrates thought of **moral reasoning** as a rational process relying mainly on logic and reasoning to approach a moral dilemma. There are typically stages that include identifying the dimensions of the moral conflict, the relevant moral principles, the relevant facts within the context of their level of importance, and then bringing these elements together to form a conclusion. Many philosophers believe that general principles of morality are essential in navigating the moral reasoning process, while some philosophers argue that virtues are essential to the process. Establishing the relevant moral facts necessary to the moral reasoning process, however, is critical.

According to **John Stuart Mill** ranking those relevant moral facts according to importance is also important. **John Rawls** (1971) on the other hand preferred a more holistic approach called **reflective equilibrium** where the decision-making process involves considering similar cases when sorting through those relevant moral facts much in the same way courts consider past cases as precedent in deciding present cases. It allows the individual who is making the decision to adapt and change their point of view through the deliberation process. Psychological theories of **moral reasoning** consider the role emotions play in the moral decision-making landscape. This contradicts Kant's view of **moral reasoning** where universal laws and the categorical imperative dictate how moral dilemmas are to be resolved and emotion is not a part of that equation.

In everyday life moral reasoning is practical relying on the constant influx of information which can change the course of the moral reasoning process. The amount of time available within which to make a moral decision will greatly impact the process itself. Police officers, for example, typically don't have the luxury of time during a crisis when balancing protecting the public against protecting the rights of individuals.

Case 3.1: Cluster Munitions
Ukraine was running low on ammunition in July, 2023 and the U.S. had to make the difficult decision of whether to send Ukraine cluster munitions. The controversy is over the use of cluster munitions as they typically result in a higher rate of civilian casualties. A cluster munition is a bomb that consists of a canister carrying smaller bombs that when detonated spread out shrapnel killing troops and destroying tanks. The problem is that not all of the smaller bombs detonate and when civilians come into contact with them later after the fighting is over then they can explode. Some countries do not allow the use of cluster munitions, but Russia, Ukraine, and the U.S. do allow using these weapons. Russia used cluster munitions in its attacks against Ukraine and the fighting all occurs within Ukrainian borders. The cluster munitions the U.S. wants to send to Ukraine have a low rate of civilian casualties as they have higher rates of the smaller bombs detonating upon initial release. And Ukraine pledged to only use the ammunition in strikes of Russian military targets, primarily away from civilian populated areas of Ukraine. Should the U.S. send cluster munitions to Ukraine? What are the conflicting moral issues? What are the moral principles that might guide the final moral conclusion? What are the relevant facts? What are the duties owed? What are the costs and benefits? What are the emotional considerations? Are there any similar cases either real or hypothetical?

Common Fallacies in Moral Reasoning

Moral reasoning is an imperfect decision-making process. Any time you've argued with someone over a moral dilemma, you've likely heard them present an argument that doesn't seem to fit logically. This avoidance of rational thought is common in moral reasoning and there are quite a few identifiable common **moral reasoning fallacies**. Some **moral reasoning fallacies** are unique to a sloppy approach within moral reasoning while others are related to the personality of the individual making the error in rational thought.

The first three **moral reasoning fallacies** we will consider can be linked to the personality of the individual who is making the argument. Someone who is rigid and not willing to keep an open mind will argue that their position is better without any real justification - a "**Mine-is-better**" approach. A second moral reasoning fallacy occurs when the individual arguing applies less stringent moral rules for themselves than they do for others, commonly known as a **double standard**. Finally, there are those who will shift focus away from their own potentially immoral reasoning by deflecting and accusing others of being just as guilty of immoral behavior. This fallacy is known as **Tu Quoque** which means "you though" in French.

The sloppy approach to moral reasoning can lead to several moral fallacies. The first involves carelessly reading into the facts of a case resulting in unwarranted assumptions. The second fallacy is similar and occurs where a case is oversimplified resulting in some of the finer details getting lost. Another related fallacy to moral reasoning occurs when people make hasty conclusions or have "knee-jerk" reactions without having all the facts to a case.

The next three fallacies involve assumptions about the law, norms, and avoiding negative outcomes. **Moral legalism** assumes that just because an act is legal, then it is moral. The best example of this concept is the fact that the law generally does not require us to be good Samaritans. While not moral, it is legal to watch someone die without intervening unless you have some duty to intervene. Similarly, just because behavior is conventional or considered to be within society's norms, does not make it moral. Slavery used to be acceptable within society's norms, but owning human beings is not moral. Finally, behavior that benefits a group or individual is not necessarily moral as a result. This is known as **moral prudentialism**. Slave owners benefited from owning slaves, but that did not make their behavior moral.

The last set of fallacies are perhaps more dangerous than the others as they appear quite reasonable on the surface. Arguably the most common fallacy might be the **slippery slope** argument that if we allow a behavior, then even worse will follow. If we legalize marijuana, then everyone will become addicted and soon we'll all be heroin and cocaine addicts. Another interesting tactic is to divert attention away from the issue at hand by raising some other issue that may not even be related to the moral dilemma being discussed. This is known as the **red herring** and is a device used to distract from the real issue. The last moral fallacy involves appealing to people's prejudices and emotions and is known as **ad populum** where the person arguing tries to invoke a mob mentality.

Case 3.2
In 2022 the U.S. Supreme Court found that the U.S. Constitution doesn't provide a right to abortion clearing the way for states to regulate abortion law. Texas now has a law that makes it a felony to perform an abortion punishable for up to life in prison. There is an exception for life-threatening medical problems, but generally doctors cannot perform abortions except in rare circumstances. Come up with some fallacies of moral reasoning with respect to the arguments for and against criminalizing abortion.

Moral Development

When and how do we become moral actors within society? **Developmental theories** are approaches to behavior proposing that individuals have normal growth phases in areas such as morality and emotional maturity. We mature physically in height and weight as charted by a pediatrician. We also mature cognitively as measured by intelligence tests and charted on a normal curve. Our emotional development is more difficult to measure but includes our ability to empathize with others and willingness to compromise our own desires with the needs of others.

Jean Piaget (2013) believed that individuals go through stages of cognitive growth that is related to their moral awareness and children develop through playing. **Lawrence Kohlberg** (1984) built off **Piaget's** work to develop a theory of moral development. **Kohlberg's** (1984) proposed **theory of moral development** has three levels each with two distinct stages. During the first two **pre-conventional stages**, the individual makes ethical decisions based on whether they will be punished and the concept of reciprocity. Decisions rest on external concerns and not standards or norms. The next two **conventional stages** are marked by moral values, right and wrong, expectations of others, maintaining social order and a sense of duty to others. The final two **post-conventional stages** are characterized by rules, legality, duty of contract, mutual trust and respect, and utilitarianism.

Kohlberg's stages of moral development have been validated across cultures, age, and gender using primarily a written instrument, sometimes combined with personal interviews. There has been some discussion in the literature regarding whether there is a gender bias in the instrument; however, testing has validated the instrument to be between 70% and 80% reliable (Kohlberg, 1984). The written instrument currently used was developed by Rest, Narvaez, Thoma and Bebeau (2000) and is known as the Defining Issues Test 2 (DIT 2).

The DIT 2 consists of three moral dilemma scenarios followed by a series of questions regarding what outcome the respondent will choose and ranking their reasoning for choosing that particular outcome. Questions are assigned scores based on how respondents rank their responses (Kohlberg, 1984). The DIT 2 has been administered to individuals of various professions and ages. Generally, as people age, as their IQ increases, and/or as they advance through their education, they progress through the stages of development.

Nolan (2000) applied **Kohlberg's stages of moral development** to police officers in Boston. The study tested new recruits, as well as seasoned officers, some who had been subjected to specialized ethics training. The findings indicated that respondents fell in the conventional stage of Kohlberg's moral development scale. There was no difference between officers who had received specialized training and those who had not in the study (Nolan, 2000). Unfortunately, the study did not explore the implications of its results with respect to police misconduct.

The Nolan dissertation did find that the police officer participants had high Stage 4 scores in Kohlberg's stages of moral development. Stage 4 is characterized by making moral decisions based on rules, laws, and regulations. Individuals who score high in stage 4 are interested in duty and social order, self-respect, and societal obligations. The Nolan dissertation also found that participant officers scored at the level of moral development equal to an American child between the ages of eleven and thirteen (Nolan, 2000).

Stewart and Sprinthall (2019) adapted Kohlberg's instrument to the public administration environment. The Stewart-Sprinthall Management Survey (SSMS) was administered to 485 public managers with most administrators falling within stage 4 and the highest stage, the principled stage, which includes stages 5 and 6. The tendency was for administrators to rely on stage 4 reasoning (Stewart & Sprinthall, 2019).

What is the significance of stage 4 moral development for public administrators? Stewart and Sprinthall (1991) observe that stage 4 development "may provide some protection against the ruthless exploitation for personal gain" or lower stage reasoning, but "it may also provide a built-in resistance to learning principled reasoning" (Stewart & Sprinthall, 1991, p. 253). Stewart and Sprinthall (1991) also note that Rohr (1978) would characterize stage 4 reasoning as "low road" decision making within administrative ethics. The next question becomes what factors influence the stages of moral development?

Studies have shown that age, IQ, occupation, and education are the biggest factors impacting an individual's progression through the stages of moral development (Rest et al., 2000). The more education one has and the older one gets, the higher the level of moral development for the average adult (Wilson et al., 1992). Some occupations foster moral development through positive mentoring practices, such as the study of medicine, resulting in the advancement of doctors through the stages of moral development (Coleman & Wilkins, 2002).

The Nolan DIT 2 results correspond with the personality characteristics found in police officers through the Myers-Briggs Type Indicator (MBTI). Lynch and McMahon (1984) found that law enforcement officers are Introverted, Sensing, Thinking and Judging (ISTJ). This combination includes individuals who are dependable, decisive, quiet, serious, thorough, detail-oriented, and logical. Sensing and Judging (SJ) individuals are responsible, duty-bound, and feel a sense of obligation within society. They are known as society's stabilizers. The SJ is talented at, "establishing policies, rules, schedules, routines, regulations and hierarchy" (Lynch & McMahon, 1984, p. 14).

It is not surprising that police work would attract individuals who are rule-oriented in their personalities and level of moral development. The selection of individuals who meet organizational expectations may influence the socialization process as those with similar attitudes will be hired making socialization within the police culture easier (Bowen et al., 1991; Kristof-Brown, 2000). What is surprising is that the moral development of police officers in the Nolan study ranked low in comparison to other professions such as enlisted men in the Navy. The Nolan study respondents ranked at the same level as prison inmates (Coleman & Wilkins, 2002).

One would hope that the hiring process would screen out questionable moral development in potential cadets. The hiring process for police officers varies greatly across the U.S. Ideally a department will take past behavior of the applicant into consideration, as well as age, IQ and education. Unfortunately, not all departments make intelligent hiring decisions. For example, one police applicant scored highly in cognitive ability during the hiring process and was denied employment on this basis (Hughes, 2003). Normally, applicants who do well on hiring tests are accepted for employment on that basis, not denied for that very reason.

Authoritarian personality has been a major concern among scholars and observers of police behavior. There are several views of the origins of **authoritarian** attitudes in police behavior. One study found that the police do not necessarily attract persons with **authoritarian** personalities (Brown & Willis, 1985). Authoritarianism may be linked to the demands placed on officers by their agency, an officer's job assignment, amount of contact with the general public, rank, and length of service (Carlson & Sutton, 1975; Lefkowitz ,1974; Genz & Lester, 1976; Hageman, 1979). Many scholars argue that police officers take on **authoritarian** personalities after less than two years on the job (Bordua, 1967). **Authoritarian** personalities are shaped by circumstances as opposed to socialization such as exposure to conflict, contact with the public, lower rank, and exposure to high crime areas. Henkel and Sheehan (1997) tested whether authoritarianism is the greatest factor influencing police misconduct. Henkel and Sheehan (1997), however, found no support in their research for the hypothesis that authoritarianism is the greatest factor influencing police misconduct. If officers do harbor **authoritarian** attitudes, there is no support that these attitudes influence their behavior.

Carol Gilligan (1983) challenged some of Kohlberg's work arguing that it lacked concepts of care and responsibility by focusing too much on impartiality as the basis for morality. In other words, how I interact with strangers is not the only way to measure morality, but how I act with people I have particular relationships with is also relevant when considering the moral self. **Gilligan** believed that moral action depended greatly on the nuances of those relationships, and she emphasized the role that emotions play in moral decision-making. **Gilligan** also rejected the notion that moral action could be universally applied to everyone, preferring a more individualistic approach.

Case 3.3: Lying and Relationships
Judy is a 12-year-old girl. Her mother promises her that she can go to see Taylor Swift at the big arena in a city nearby if she saves up from baby-sitting to buy a ticket to the concert. Judy manages to save up more than the ticket cost, but then her mother changes her mind and tells Judy that she must spend the money on new clothes for school. Judy is disappointed and decides to go to the concert anyway. She buys a ticket, puts her extra babysitting money aside for buying new clothes, and tells her mother that she is spending the night over at her friend's house on the night of the concert. A week passes without her mother finding out. Judy then tells her older sister, Louise, that she went to the concert and lied to their mother about it. Louise wonders whether to tell their mother about what Judy did. Consider Judy's decision to lie, the mother's decision to break the promise, and Louise's dilemma over whether to tell their mother about Judy's lie. What are the relevant facts? What impact does Judy's age have on her decision to lie? Does her older sister have a different duty because of her age and/or her role as a sister? What impact does the fact that the mother made a promise have with respect to Judy lying and/or Louise telling their mother about the lie?

Deviant Behavior and Delinquency

What are the causes of immoral behavior? Sociological theories regarding crime and delinquency provide a perspective relevant to adolescent delinquent behavior. While deviant behavior theories are traditionally used to explain crime, deviant behavior does not have to be criminal behavior. It can be any behavior considered deviant from social norms (Kornhauser, 1978). There are many sociological theories purporting to explain deviant behavior, however, two main theories are the basis for many other deviant behavior theories - **Differential Association Theory (DAT)** and **Social Control Theory (SCT)**.

Edwin Sutherland is considered the father of **DAT**. *Principles of Criminology,* Sutherland's seminal work on the subject, was first published in 1934 and is currently in its 11th edition despite Sutherland's death in 1950 (Sutherland et al., 1970). According to Sutherland in **DAT** criminal behavior is learned in intimate relationships and personal groups. Individuals commit crime when they have learned "an excess of definitions favorable to law violation over definitions unfavorable to law violation" (Matsueda quoting Sutherland, 1982). Essentially, through communication within groups, individuals learn techniques, motives, and rationalizations for committing deviant acts.

Definitions favorable to crime are weighted by the frequency, duration, priority, and intensity of relationships within personal groups. Cultural deviance theory is a result of culture and subculture supporting norms that are different from those of society. A culture or subculture exists, recruits new members, establishes norms that conflict with the norms of society at large, and supports criminalized behavior. This encouragement of criminal behavior causes delinquency and crime (Kornhauser, 1978).

Based on a review of Sutherland's theory, Matsueda (1982) identifies five relevant variables of causal relationships within a **DAT** model. These variables include background, parental supervision, peer relationships, definitions favorable/unfavorable to crime, and delinquency. According to **DAT**, an individual's background, relationships with peers, and parental supervision shape whether the individual will develop definitions favorable or unfavorable to crime. An individual's background will also determine the way in which they are supervised and the types of peers with whom they associate.

There are several fundamental differences between **DAT** and **SCT**. First, **DAT** asserts that criminal behavior is learned, not innate, as this chapter will explore in the next section. Second, **DAT** stresses the importance of subcultures through the overwhelming influence of peers on criminal behavior, which is the exact opposite of **SCT**. Finally, **DAT** focuses on the importance of culture overall as influential to the formation of definitions ultimately leading to delinquent behavior. Not all social theorists subscribe to differential association theory. Some social scientists argue that the potential for deviant behavior is within each of us.

If Sutherland is the father of **DAT**, then Travis Hirschi may be the father of **SCT**. Hirschi, relying on Durkheim, Hobbes, Matza and others, brought attention to this theory of criminal behavior in his 1969 *Causes of Delinquency*. According to Hirschi with **SCT** we are all born delinquent, but controls within society constrain our behavior. Constraints on behavior can be internal or external, direct or indirect (Kornhauser, 1978). Social bonds, particularly to parents, have the greatest impact on whether individuals will commit deviant acts (Hirschi, 2002).

Hirschi describes these social bonds as attachment, commitment, involvement, and belief. Attachment to parents, school and peers "assumes that the bond of affection for conventional persons is a major deterrent to crime" (Hirschi, 1969, p. 83). Attachment can be measured by the amount of supervision and communication between the adult and the adolescent, the amount of contact with the peer, or the performance in school. Commitment refers to the stake the adolescent has in conformity within society which can be measured by the frequency with which they engage in adult behaviors such as smoking, dating, and drinking alcohol. Involvement in conventional activities is measured through homework and hobbies while belief in values and norms are measured in attitudes toward law enforcement, delinquents, and victims (Hirschi, 1969). Hirschi argues that variables measuring behavior are preferable when testing control theories (Hirschi, 1990).

Attachments constrain behavior, according to Hirschi, keeping people from committing delinquent behavior out of fear. In Hirschi's model, there is a hypothesized attachment to peers and parents for delinquency. Hirschi asserts that attachment can cause delinquency by influencing belief in a single moral order, leading to delinquency through lack of supervision. According to SCT, peers are not important, but parents are very important. Delinquents are unable to become attached to anyone, social controls are weak, and delinquents are then able to act out their innate desire to commit delinquent acts (Hirschi, 1969; Kornhauser, 1978).

Another sociological theory, **Control Balance Theory (CBT)**, suggests that deviance is a result of an imbalance between three key variables, which include motivation, constraint, and opportunity (Tittle, 1995). One study utilized officer misconduct scenarios administered to officers in Philadelphia. The results were analyzed to determine whether the amount of control that officers are subject to in relationship to the amount of control they have in their environment affects their decision to report peer misconduct (Hickman et al., 2001). The Hickman et al. (2001) study relies on Tittle's (1995) **CBT**. This theory is based on the potential deviant becoming aware of an imbalance of control in a given situation and using deviant behavior in order to regain control over the situation (Tittle, 1995). The Hickman et al. (2001) study did show a relationship such that officers with less control over the situation were more likely to report peer misconduct.

Case 3.4: Relationships and Degrees of Harm
Two young men who are brothers have gotten into some serious trouble and need to leave town quickly, but they need some money before they leave. Karl, the older one, broke into a store and stole a thousand dollars. Bob, the younger one, went to a retired old man who was known to help people in town. He told the man that he was very sick and that he needed a thousand dollars to pay for medical bills. Bob asked the old man to lend him the money and promised that he would pay him back when he recovered. Really Bob wasn't sick at all, and he had no intention of paying the man back. Although the old man didn't know Bob very well, he lent him the money. So, Bob and Karl skipped town, each with a thousand dollars. Which is worse, stealing like Karl or cheating like Bob? Why is that worse? Is it important to keep a promise to someone you don't know well or will never see again? Why or why not? Was the old man being irresponsible by lending Bob the money? Why or why not?

Conclusion

The story of Judy lying to her mother so she could go to a Taylor Swift concert is an adaptation of one of Kohlberg's moral development scenarios used to measure where we fall within the scale he developed. The story of Karl and Bob stealing money and skipping town is another Kohlberg scenario. These scenarios highlight the importance of considering relationships, duties, and promises within the moral reasoning process. The importance of these scenarios is as much about what moral decision you come to as it is about your moral reasoning in coming to that decision.

Perhaps the most well-known Kohlberg scenario involves a man trying to buy expensive medicine for his dying wife and a druggist who is unwilling to cut him a break. While Kohlberg's scenarios were developed decades ago, the problems he presents and the issues he raises are still very relevant today. Rising healthcare costs and the lack of adequate medical insurance can cause people to lose everything they have, forcing the individual facing this type of dilemma into making hard choices. Moral reasoning is our mechanism for facing these types of dilemmas.

Debate Topics for In-Class Discussion

1. Increasing restrictions on gun sales in the U.S.
    a. *Pro* – restrictions protect the public and provide law enforcement a way to track and control gun sales thus limiting the use of guns in illegal activity
    b. *Con* – limiting gun sales further pushes the sale of guns onto a black market, making detection and control more difficult
2. Legalizing marijuana
    a. *Pro* – provides easy access to a drug that is not much different than alcohol, reduces the focus on criminalizing the use and sale of marijuana which frees up the criminal justice system

b. *Con* – because regulations for growing marijuana can be strict it encourages many to grow marijuana illegally and avoid the regulations which then can cause other problems including environmental issues; also the federal government does not recognize the legalization of marijuana making it a conflict of laws

Terms

Socratic method
Moral reasoning
Hume's Law
Cost-benefit analysis
John Stuart Mill
John Rawls
Moral reasoning fallacies
Double standard
Tu Quoque
Moral legalism
Moral prudentialism
Slippery slope
Red herring
Ad populum
Jean Piaget
Lawrence Kohlberg
Kohlberg's stages of moral development
Pre-conventional stages
Conventional stages
Post-conventional stages
Carol Gilligan
Differential Association Theory (DAT)
Social Control Theory (SCT)
Control Balance Theory (CBT)
Reflective Equilibrium
Mine-is-better
Developmental theories
Authoritarian

References

Bordua, D. J. (Ed.). (1967). *The police: Six sociological essays.* New York: Wiley.

Bowen, D.E., Ledford Jr., G.E., & Nathan, B.R. (1991). Hiring for the Organization, Not the Job. *Academy of Management Executive, 5*(4), 35-51.

Brown, L., & Willis, A. (1985). Authoritarianism in British Police Recruits - Importation, Socialization or Myth. *Journal of Occupational Psychology, 58*(2), 97-108.

Carlson, H.M., & Sutton, M.S. (1975). The Effects of Different Police Roles on Attitudes and Values. *The Journal of Psychology, 91,* 57-64.

Coleman, R., & Wilkins, L. (2002). Searching for the ethical journalist: An exploratory study of the moral development of news workers. *Journal of Mass Media Ethics, 17*(3), 209-225.

Genz, J.L., & Lester, D. (1976). Authoritarianism in Policemen as a Function of Experience. *Journal of Police Science and Administration, 4,* 9-13.

Gilligan, C. (1983). Do the social sciences have an adequate theory of moral development?. In *Social science as moral inquiry* (pp. 33-51). Columbia University Press.

Hageman, M.J. (1979). Who Joins the Force for What Reasons: An Argument for "The New Breed". *Journal of Police Science and Administration, 7,* 206-210.

Henkel, J., & Sheehan, E.P. (1997). Relation of Police Misconduct to Authoritarianism. *Journal of Social Behavior & Personality, 12*(2), 551-556.

Hickman, M.J., Piquero, A.R., Lawton, B.A., & Greene, J.R. (2001). Applying Tittle's Control Balance Theory to Police Deviance. *Policing: An International Journal of Police Strategies and Management,* 24(4), 497-519.

Hirschi, T. (1969). *Causes of Delinquency.* (ed.). Berkeley: University of California Press.

Hirschi, T., & Gottfredson, M. *A General Theory of Crime.* Stanford University Press: Stanford (1990).

Hughes, T.T. (2003). Jordan v. The City of New London, Police Hiring and IQ. *Policing: An International Journal of Police Strategies and Management, 26*(2), 298-312.

Hume, D. (1739). *Treatise of Human Nature.* London: John Noon.

Kohlberg, L. (1984). *The psychology of moral development: The nature and validity of moral sages.* New York, NY: Harper & Row.

Kornhauser, R.R. (1978). *Social Sources of Delinquency.* (ed.). Chicago: University of Chicago Press.

Kristof-Brown, A.L. (2000). Perceived Applicant Fit: Distinguishing Between Recruiters' Perceptions of Person-Job and Person-Organization Fit. *Personnel Psychology, 53*(3), 643-671.

Lefkowitz, J. (1974). Job Attitudes of Police: Overall Description and Demographic Correlates. *Journal of Vocational Behavior, 5,* 221-230.

Lynch, R.G., & McMahon, R.R. (1984). *Getting to Know Policemen Personally.* (ed.). Chapel Hill: Institute of Government.

Matsueda, R. (1982). Testing Control Theory and Differential Association: A Causal Modeling Approach. *American Sociological Review, 47*(4), 489-504.

Nolan, T.W. (2000). *Toward Probity: The Moral Milieu of the Police Station House.* Boston University.

Piaget, J. (2013). *The moral judgment of the child.* Routledge.

Rawls, J. (1971). *A Theory of Justice,* 2nd Edition 1999, Cambridge, MA: Harvard University Press.

Rest, J.R., Narvaez, D., Thoma, S.J., & Bebeau, M.J. (2000). A neo-Kohlbergian approach to morality research. *Journal of Moral Education, 29*(4), 381-395.

Rohr, J.A. (1978). *Ethics for Bureaucrats: An Essay on Law and Values.* New York: Marcel Dekker.

Stewart, D. W., Sprinthall, N. W., & Shafer, D. M. (2019). Moral development in public administration. *Handbook of administrative ethics,* 457-480.

Stewart, D. W., & Sprinthall, N. A. (1991). Strengthening ethical judgment in public administration. *Ethical frontiers in public management,* 243-260.

Sutherland, E.H., Cressey, D.R., & Luckenbill, D.F. (1970). *Principles of Criminology.* (ed.). Philadelphia: Lippincott.

Tittle, C.R. (1995). *Control Balance: Toward a General Theory of Deviance (Crime and Society).* (ed.). New York: Westview Press.

Wilson, K.L., Rest, J.R., Boldizar, J.P., & Deemer, D.K. (1992). Moral Judgment Development: The Effects of Education and Occupation. *Social Justice Research, 5*(1), 31-48.

Chapter 4
Administrative Ethics

Chapter Objectives

1. Expose students to some of the causes of unethical behavior in street-level bureaucrats.
2. Discuss concepts of organizational deviance and administrative evil.
3. Recognize the impact discretion has on the work of bureaucrats within the criminal justice system.
4. Explore elements of bureaucratic organizational culture theories.

Introduction

Post Word War II, society pledged to keep the atrocities of the Holocaust from happening again. Unfortunately, accusations of ethnic cleansing and genocide continue to occur globally. In Bosnia in the early to mid-1990s, Muslims were targeted by the Bosnian government and over 8,000 Muslim Bosnian citizens were killed with thousands more displaced from their homes. In Darfur, armed militias continually wipe out entire villages forcing the evacuation of over 1.2 million residents between April and October of 2023 (Landale, 2023). And Russia may have committed genocide when it kidnapped children from Ukraine, forcing them to be assimilated into Russian families if their intent was to destroy Ukraine's ethnic identity. None of these atrocities is possible without the coordination of street-level bureaucrats like police officers, soldiers, and administrators.

Individuals who work within the criminal justice system are administrators or bureaucrats. They work in the public sector and face some of the same moral dilemmas that anyone within the private sector might face, but with some differences given the nature of their work.

Just like in the public sector, their standards and institutionalized norms contribute to socialization within their respective organizations. The following section reviews factors impacting the street-level bureaucrat's ethical decision-making process.

Background

The questions analyzed by this chapter are fundamental to administrative ethics.

1. What are the differences in ethical attitudes and behavior in street-level bureaucrats and what causes these differences?
2. Do civil servants come to public service with strong public service values?
3. Are bureaucrats socialized within their agency to commit unethical acts or to uphold ethical standards?
4. Are bureaucrats exposed to such stressful and/or unusual working conditions that it inevitably leads to erosion of their commitment to ethical behavior, or do they choose to remain more committed in their ethical values?
5. Is the ethical behavior of civil servants shaped by the attitudes of peers and the actions of their agency?
6. Which of these issues has the greatest impact on the ethical behavior of civil servants?

What are the **causes of unethical behavior by street-level bureaucrats** within public administration? That small percentage of civil servants who do commit unethical acts during their careers may not be screened during recruitment. Another possibility is that the job itself attracts people of a certain personality type and/or disposition that is conducive to abandoning public service values when the right conditions exist. The minimum requirements for hiring individuals may be inadequate by allowing inexperienced, young individuals into a career at a stage of moral development that is not appropriate for their job in public service. As we have seen, all adults have a level of moral development that reflects in part their experience. Most of the population has moral reasoning based on conventional stages of moral development that are guided by moral values, understanding the difference between what is right and what is wrong, maintaining social order and a sense of duty to others (Kohlberg, 1984).

An alternative possibility is that young bureaucrats have good intentions but have weakly formed ethical attitudes and a naive view of their work. They may be subject to the influence of peers and become disillusioned and "hardened" by conditions they encounter within their agency. Their level of moral development before joining their agency will affect how they respond to ethical challenges. Socialization on-the-job, the process by which civil servants learn group values and established behaviors, will affect their level of moral development after joining their agency and will alter how they respond to ethical challenges (Lundman, 1980).

Public servants who come to public service with strong public service values may still be ultimately socialized to commit unethical acts through training, peers, and supervisors. Public administrators are greatly impacted by peers and supervisors with respect to their attitudes towards misconduct. Their values may be reinforced with professional ethical norms and organizational practices. If the organizational norms of an agency support unethical behavior, then eventually bureaucrats will either quit their job out of frustration, join in the undesirable behavior, or alienate themselves from their fellow peers who may be engaging in unethical conduct (Hirschman, 1970). The individual's relationship with his/her peers and supervisors will greatly impact which direction the bureaucrat chooses.

It is also important to consider the factors that contribute to a bureaucrat's ability to commit unethical acts. It is difficult, if not impossible, to monitor someone in their job daily. Most street-level bureaucrats enjoy a great deal of autonomy in their jobs. Discretion does not automatically lead to unethical acts and is necessary for bureaucrats to effectively carry out their jobs. However, it does allow the opportunity for unethical acts to occur.

Those who can report misbehavior - the citizens who perceive that they have been mistreated - are at a disadvantage on several levels. For example, within the criminal justice system most of the citizens who would be prone to complaining are in the process of being arrested, convicted, or incarcerated and as such the veracity of their claims is suspect at best. Those that might complain are faced with the fear of reprisal. There is also some skepticism on the part of the citizen who feels that such complaints will fall on deaf ears (Maynard-Moody & Musheno, 2000). In some instances, supervisors who wish to protect their employees do in fact ignore such complaints.

In both private business and public agencies, **codes of ethics** are considered a part of the culture. It is treated similarly to a mission statement - a means of communicating the ethical mandates prescribed by the corporation or agency (Simon, 1995). For example, the current Police Code of Conduct was originally a resolution passed in 1957 at the annual International Association of Chiefs of Police (IACP) conference. The code was not altered again until the 1989 IACP conference. Further changes were made to the code and the result was the creation of both the Law Enforcement Code of Ethics and the Police Code of Conduct, which were approved by the IACP in 1991 at their annual conference. These are the formal ethical standards of police officers. Whether officers follow these formal constraints, however, depends on a multitude of factors within their working environment.

Case 4.1: Screening Police Officers
Many police agencies require polygraph tests, as well as personality testing as a condition of employment even though neither are considered reliable in terms of predicting future behavior. Should we rely on polygraph tests and/or personality testing in employment within the criminal justice system? If so, how much weight do we give to these diagnostic type tools? Are there better ways to screen future employees?

Causes of Unethical Behavior in Street-Level Bureaucrats

According to Michael Lipsky (1980), street-level bureaucrats face many challenges that can potentially lead to unethical behavior in public agencies. Resources, clients, goals, performance measures, alienation, discretion, hiring, training, personality, supervisors, and coworkers each contribute to the street-level bureaucrat's ethical decision-making. For the street-level bureaucrat, generally, resources are limited, clients are non-voluntary, goals are ambiguous and performance measures are inadequate. The street-level bureaucrat has a great deal of discretion in carrying out his/her mission. Ultimately, the organizational culture, and in particular the attitudes and behavior of supervisors and coworkers, will impact how the street-level bureaucrat handles all these issues.

Street-level bureaucrats enormously influence the public's lives every day. Agencies provide public benefits and have the authority to sanction the public. In essence, bureaucrats "hold the keys to a dimension of citizenship" (Lipsky, 1980, p. 4). Unfortunately, the essential work bureaucrats perform is subject to conditions that hinder the effective and efficient delivery of services. For example, police officers certainly face all these dilemmas in public service including a lack of resources, ambiguous and conflicting goals, strained community relations, and inadequate ways of measuring their job performance. These problems, coupled with the constant threat of violence, make for an extremely stressful work environment.

Bureaucrats are faced with **limited resources** that are generally inadequate to fulfil the requirements of their jobs. Should additional resources be made available, the public immediately uses them up, constantly hungering for more services. In other words, demand will inevitably catch up with supply. This cycle eventually brings the agency back to its original position. Jails and prisons have faced constant overcrowding no matter how many new facilities are built. Constantly facing inadequate resources is stressful and places a great amount of pressure on the bureaucrat's time. It also creates conflict as agencies must meet Constitutional requirements of equity. They must provide the same level of protection to each citizen when providing services to the community (Lipsky, 1980).

Working with this lack of resources, bureaucrats must face **non-voluntary clients** with whom they may experience conflict. This friction between bureaucrats and clients makes it difficult sometimes to carry out the bureaucrat's tasks. One factor affecting this relationship is the fact that clients are usually not included as a reference group for bureaucrats, which greatly impacts the way in which services are delivered. Defendants aren't typically consulted when attorneys and judges decide how their courts will operate, for example. Ultimately, this allows the bureaucrat the ability to abuse the bureaucrat/client relationship given that the client cannot walk away from the transaction (Lipsky, 1980).

Lipsky (1980) argues that bureaucrats have **ambiguous goals** and **inadequate performance measurement** given that their tasks revolve around public service. Goals can be diverse and contradictory like an officer's goal of protecting the public which conflicts with aggressive police tactics for controlling crime. The more ambiguous and contradictory the goals, the more important the relationship between bureaucrats and their co-workers is to sustain morale at work. Lack of supervisory monitoring contributes to the inadequacy of performance measurement. Agencies are forced to use surrogate measures for performance measurement. This can cause bureaucrats to channel their focus in unintended ways.

Lipsky (1980) points out that street-level bureaucratic work is **alienated work**. "Jobs that require workers to deny the basic humanity of others" can be considered alienating work. This results in the bureaucrat becoming "less concerned with protecting clients' interests and their own connection with clients" (Lipsky, 1980, p. 79). Alienated workers can become dissatisfied with their jobs which leads to absenteeism and less than adequate job performance.

Case 4.2: Performance Measures
Lipsky points out that measuring the performance of public service workers is difficult which can lead to focusing on surrogate measures. For example, officers are often measured by their number of arrests, number of citations given out, and numbers of calls for service they respond to. What do these measures tell us about an officer's performance on-the-job? What are the limitations of these measures? What other measures should be considered when evaluating an officer's job performance?

Discretion

Discretion is inevitable for the street-level bureaucrat (Maynard-Moody & Musheno, 2000). Police officers enjoy high levels of **discretion** given the nature of their job. Does **discretion** automatically lead to abuse? Are tighter controls and supervision the answer? One problem with tighter controls is that it causes abuse to become more secretive and harder to find. There are existing controls that allow street-level workers to self-monitor. They also rely on peers, supervisors, and clients to keep themselves in check (Maynard-Moody & Musheno, 2000). As Lipsky (1980) points out, "discretion provides opportunity to intervene on behalf of clients as well as to discriminate among them" (Lipsky, 1980, p. 23). Discretion, then, can provide flexibility for bureaucrats and limiting discretion can create as many problems as it solves.

Within the police force it is difficult, if not impossible, given the nature of the work to significantly increase supervision in as much as the officer works alone (Lipsky, 1980). In addition to self-control, officers rely on peers and the complaints from the public to keep them in check. Relying on these resources, however, raises further problems. For example, citizens have difficulty reporting police misconduct (Maynard-Moody & Musheno, 2000). Furthermore, peers can also be corrupt leading to the corrupt socialization of officers on-the-job (Lundman, 1980).

A 2000 survey reveals that approximately 95% of police departments in the U.S. have currently adopted community policing (LEMAS, 2000). Community policing allows policing to retain its autonomous characteristics. This autonomy, in turn, allows officers the opportunity to commit deviant acts. However, discretion alone does not mean that an officer will automatically turn to deviant behavior.

Maynard-Moody and Musheno (2000) seek to analyze street-level work **discretion** from two different perspectives or views. The first is called the **dominant view** or **state-agent narrative** which says that self-interest is the guiding force behind decisions. The counter narrative is that of the **citizen agent** who is responsive to the needs of the client, basing decisions on their administrative experience.

The **dominant view** sees street-level workers as policymakers whose job is to execute the laws the government passes. This view says that the street-level worker relies on self-interest in decision-making - i.e.: what will make my life easier and what will get this case out of my life faster? This view acknowledges that sometimes the street-level worker will go above and beyond the call of duty - picking a small number of cases that seem worthy to give special attention to, but that the worker doesn't have the time or the resources to do so with every case. The **citizen-agent view** sees the street-level worker as responsive to clients, experienced, relying on normative values rather than rules, distrustful of politicians and supervisors who only create obstacles to helping the client. This is a view that street-level workers themselves hold (Maynard-Moody & Musheno, 2000).

One example found in Maynard-Moody and Musheno's (2000) research involves a woman who comes to the police department to complain about the police roughing up her husband when mistakenly arresting him. The woman had to pray for several days before coming in because the original incident was so frightening to her. In the first instance of police discretion, the police used discretion to brutalize her husband. In the second instance, the police officer within the department hearing the woman's concerns used his discretion to help the woman file a formal complaint (Maynard-Moody & Musheno, 2000).

Lieutenant Ken Adcox (2000) of the El Paso Police Department points out that both line officers and managers exercise discretion in their jobs. Adcox (2000) focuses on the unsupervised line officer making quick decisions with "immense autonomy and latitude" (Adcox, 2000, p. 17). While Adcox (2000) recognizes the necessity of police discretion, relying on Lewis (1991), Adcox (2000) also recognizes the subsequent potential for unethical behavior. Judges, lawyers, and corrections officers are much the same, making quick decisions every day within the context of their work.

Case 4.3: Citizen Complaints
Maynard-Moody and Musheno raise the issue of how difficult it can be for citizens to complain about unethical officer behavior. What can be done to make it easier for citizens to bring their concerns regarding an officer to an agency? What impact has Body Worn Cameras (BWC) had on complaints against officers? What about the use of cellphone videos?

Organizational Corruption

Organizational corruption focuses on an agency culture where individuals within the organization accept unethical acts. Unethical bureaucrats are protected, and whistleblowers are not only discouraged, but also punished for coming forward (Caiden & Caiden, 1977). For **organizational deviance** to occur, there must be several conditions present. The deviant acts must violate norms and/or rules accepted outside of an agency while being supported within the formal goals and rules within an agency. Recruitment, socialization, peers, and supervisors must all support these internal operating norms of deviant behavior. These conditions combined support organizational deviance (Lundman, 1980).

This theory of **organizational deviance** found partial support when tested using citizen complaints against police officers with respect to the use of physical force. The study found that field training, in-service training, length of service, arrest rate, and the population size served each had an impact on the number of citizen complaints. Departments that had field training and in-service training regarding use of force had lower citizen complaint rates. The longer an officer served, the lower the complaint rate. Also, departments serving larger populations and with higher arrest rates experienced higher citizen complaint rates (Cao et al., 2000).

Entire police agencies and correctional facilities have been accused of corruption and some have had the Department of Justice (DOJ) investigate them. Where systemic corruption within an agency is found, the court will force the agency to enter into a **consent decree**. This is a legal agreement between the DOJ and the agency whereby the agency agrees to perform required activities designed to correct corrupt behavior. The DOJ monitors the agency to ensure that the terms of the agreement are being met.

Organizational factors such as size of agency, departmental bureaucratization, and police presence or the number of police officers patrolling within a community, have also been found to affect officer behavior (Klinger, 2004). Organizational structure can also influence the ethical orientation of police officers. Van Wart (1998) argues, "organizational values are embedded in the organizational design" (Van Wart, 1998, p. 15). Some deviant behavior happens as a result of a concerted effort of many individuals within an organization, supported by organizational internal norms, peers and supervisors. The hierarchical structure of an organization can also impact behavior within the organization. For example, Kraska and Kappeler (1997) attribute the military model with the creation of an environment that fosters the use of force.

There are essentially three primary similarities between military and police organizations. First, both institutions are highly structured, hierarchical command organizations. Each uses the same basic chain of command hierarchical structure, which relies on rank for authority. Coupled with this similarity is the fact that both use similar jargon such as the names of rank and position. Finally, both institutions have similar communication structures. Each sees the flow of information within the organization as unidirectional - flowing from the top down through the hierarchy of authority (Hodgson, 2001). The reason the military and law enforcement are so similar is a result of the direct involvement the military has had in law enforcement historically. Even today, law enforcement is directly impacted by the military. Since their inception in the mid 1960's, there has been a sharp increase in the number of Special Weapons and Tactical (SWAT) teams that are military units (Weber, 1999).

Some scholars have examined the impact of size, although the findings are not conclusive. Etzioni (1975) and Slovak (1988) indicate that larger police departments result in coercive measures toward the public they serve due to a lack of adequate supervision. Chatterton (1983) adds that officers in large departments can become disconnected resulting in deviant behavior on the job. Other research demonstrates differences in behavior but does not attempt to show whether variations are inappropriate. The arrest rates for driving under the influence in very small agencies (five or fewer officers) were three times higher than arrest rates in large agencies (100 or more officers) (Mastrofski & Ritti, 1996). On the other hand, research conducted in the 1970's showed that officers in larger agencies tended to arrest and use force more often than their counterparts in smaller agencies (Klinger, 2004). According to these studies, it is not clear whether the size of agency has a consistent impact on behavior.

Case 4.4: Bystander Intervention
Mandated by a consent decree, the Ethical Policing is Courageous (EPIC) program was developed by the New Orleans Police Department (NOPD) (Consent Decree, 2013). The EPIC curriculum is based on active bystandership, encouraging officers to intervene when police misconduct could potentially occur. How difficult do you believe it will be to get officers to intervene when one of their peers is engaging in unethical behavior? Have you ever intervened when you've seen something unethical happening? If so, what motivated you to intervene?

Administrative Evil

Administrative evil occurs when ordinary people commit horrible acts by simply following orders within the scope of their employment. It doesn't seem possible that ordinary people would voluntarily commit evil acts without realizing what they're doing, however, one possible rationalization is that "Most of our daily life in social institutions and organizations is taken for granted" (Adams & Balfour, 1998, p. 19). Where organizational goals and proper authority exist within an agency, the administrator's discretion in making value judgments is removed. **Administrative evil** occurs when administrators forget what history has shown, repackage something evil and define it as good. Administrators who forget their purpose and/or abandon their sense of accountability through neutral competence can cause great public harm (Adams & Balfour, 1998).

One example of **administrative evil** is the case of the Holocaust. Most people think of Adolf Hitler as the sole cause of the Holocaust; however, he had many civil servants working across Germany who indirectly supported the functioning of the country through their work. Most administrators:

> were relatively comfortable in positions that entailed 'morally neutral' functions, such as economic affairs, tax collection, social

> security, statistics, railroad service, foreign currency, municipal government, and so forth... (Adams & Balfour, 1998, p. 46)

In order to perpetuate the holocaust, a variety of administrators were needed to process Jews into concentration camps including soldiers, administrators, and train conductors.

An example of how this everyday work supported the Holocaust would be best illustrated by a failure in the sewage system at Auschwitz which was built with an inadequate number of resources. Engineers were brought to Auschwitz to design and build a new sewage system. Although these engineers never directly participated in the murders at Auschwitz, they contributed to the overall functioning of the camp making it possible for activities at the camp to continue. The Holocaust could not have succeeded without the many bureaucrats keeping the various necessary components functioning.

One danger of **administrative evil** is our slowness to respond to and eventually learn from the failures of the past. Researchers continually learn more about administrative evil in events like the Holocaust, the *Challenger* and *Columbia* disasters, and the relocation of the Japanese during World War II. Studying the factors that lead up to a disaster or an event like the Holocaust is made more difficult because, "Genocide is a controversial topic that may very well pit the researcher against the state" (Adams & Balfour, 1998, p. 7).

Researchers attempting to draw conclusions about atrocities like the Holocaust must critique any government or agency who may have been involved. This critique can be especially difficult when the researcher is criticizing agencies and governments within their own country of residence. As a result, some researchers struggle to pose the hard-hitting questions that are necessary to understand all the dimensions of how genocide or some other man-made disaster occurred.

With **administrative evil**, individuals can unintentionally commit acts of evil more easily when they believe they are simply doing their job. This idea is often reinforced using euphemisms.

> In cases of moral inversion, euphemism or technical language can enable us to disconnect our actions from our normal, moral categories of right and wrong, good and evil. (Adams & Balfour, 1998, p. 18)

For example, during the Holocaust, words like "killing" were replaced with words and phrases like "evacuation," "special treatment," and "the final solution." Language is used to dehumanize people, fostering a conducive environment for administrative evil to thrive. By calling a population of people "pests" or "rodents," they are not only dehumanized, but they are also turned into a surplus population. In this way Jews were made to look harmful providing a rationale for "removal."

Case 4.5: Administrative Evil
In 1986, the Space Shuttle Challenger broke apart within the first couple of minutes after launch killing the entire crew. A fatal flaw that could potentially occur in cold weather launches in some of the parts caused the explosion. Engineers warned of these technical concerns, but their managers did not pass the information along to the relevant supervisors. If you were an engineer and you passed these warnings along to your manager, would you feel comfortable going to their supervisor? What do you think the result might be if you did? Who bears the ultimate responsibility for this failure causing the loss of human life? What do you think the consequences should be in this case?

Culture

Wilson (1989) explains that bureaucratic behavior depends upon the bureaucratic **culture**, which includes "the situations they encounter, their prior experiences and personal beliefs, the expectations of their peers, and the array of interests in which their agency is embedded"

(Wilson, 1989, p. 27). There are numerous definitions of **culture**. Most definitions highlight the importance of attitudes, as well as the situation-dependent nature of bureaucratic behavior. Paoline (2001) utilizes a culmination of various definitions including "attitudes and values that are shared and socially transmitted among groups of people, in an attempt to cope with common problems and/or situations" (Paoline, 2001, p. 7). Van Wart (1998) defines **professional culture** as one that is "expressed in norms, symbols, and a worldview" (Van Wart, 1998, p. 63). Police officers, lawyers, and correctional officers each have their own bureaucratic culture within their respective agencies.

There are other public administration theories regarding **public sector culture** including one theory that identifies four types of organizational culture and the impact each has on its members. These four types include rational cultures, hierarchical cultures, group or team cultures, and adaptive cultures. These organizational culture types are derived from the **competing values approach (CVA)** developed by Quinn and Rohrbaugh (1981). **CVA** is a framework that argues where values compete within an organization, there is conflict. When an organization favors one value it is to the detriment of the corresponding competing value (Quinn & Rohrbaugh, 1981). In a court system where plea agreements are valued, this will come at the expense of protecting a defendant's right to a trial as all members of the organization will push towards achieving high numbers of plea agreements.

Buenger et al. (1996) tested Quinn and Rohrbaugh's competing values within the Air Force. The study found support for **CVA**. Where an agency placed emphasis on one value, the corresponding competing value received less attention than its counterpart. Previous studies have found support for **CVA** in modeling organizational forms and studying leadership styles (Quinn & Rohrbaugh, 1981; Quinn & Hall, 1983; Quinn, 1984).

Case 4.6: Corporate Culture
Imagine you're a new employee in an agency with a toxic work environment. For example, what if your boss is erratic, being kind one moment and then chastising employees the next over very small mistakes. The impact is that the other employees constantly complain about the boss. What does that mean to you – to be in a toxic work environment? How can you overcome the toxic work environment? How does being a new employee impact your ability to adapt and/or change that environment? What can change that type of environment?

Conclusion

The fundamental questions posed at the beginning of this chapter come down to the values and attitudes of public servants and whether they feel they owe certain duties to the public they serve. How they come to those values – through socialization while on-the-job or in their upbringing prior to public service employment – is important to their ethical decision-making as is their exposure to stressful work conditions and the attitudes of their peers.

Debate Topics for In-Class Discussion

1. Whether officers have a college degree for employment
    a. *Pro* – advanced education will create a more professional force and could lead to a reduction in unnecessary use of force complaints
    b. *Con* – it's challenging to find college graduates who want to go into police work which would then severely limit hiring pools
2. Community Review Boards
    a. *Pro* – provides a mechanism for members of the community to hold agencies accountable and to have a voice in how those agencies function
    b. *Con* – often these boards don't have the power to change anything, only to make recommendations which greatly limits their impact; they also don't have the expertise of the

individuals who work in those agencies putting them at a disadvantage in terms of evaluating an individual's behavior within the context of their jobs

Terms

Causes of unethical behavior by street-level bureaucrats
Codes of ethics
Limited resources
Non-voluntary clients
Ambiguous goals
Inadequate performance measurement
Alienated work
Discretion
Dominant view/State-agent narrative
Citizen agent
Organizational corruption/Organizational deviance
Consent decree
Administrative Evil
Culture
Professional culture
Public sector culture
Competing Values Approach (CVA)

References

Adams, G.B., & Balfour, D.L. (1998). *Unmasking Administrative Evil.* Thousand Oaks: Sage Publications.

Adcox, K.L. (2000, January). Doing Bad Things for Good Reasons. *The Police Chief,* 17-28.

Buenger, V., Daft, R.L., Conlon, E.J., & Austin, J. (1996). Competing Values in Organizations: Contextual Influences and Structural Consequences. *Organization Science, 7*(5), 557-576.

Caiden, G.E., & Caiden, N.J. (1977). Developments in Research: Administrative Corruption. *Public Administration Review,* 301-309.

Cao, L., Deng, X., & Barton, S. (2000). A test of Lundman's organizational product thesis with data on citizen complaints. *Policing: An International Journal of Police Strategies and Management, 23*(3), 356-373.

Chatterton, M. (1983). *Police Work and Assault Charges in the Police Organization*. (ed.). Cambridge, MA: MIT Press.

Consent Decree Regarding the New Orleans Police Department. (2012). Retrieved from http://www.laed.uscourts.gov/Consent/NewOrleans Decree.pdf

Etzioni, A. (1975). *A Comparative Analysis of Complex Organizations*. (ed.). New York, NY: Free Press.

Hirschman, A.O. (1970). Exit, Voice and Loyalty: Responses to Decline in Firms, Organizations and States. (ed.). Boston: Harvard University Press.

Hodgson, J.F. (2001). Police Violence in Canada and the USA: Analysis and Management. *Policing: An International Journal of Police Strategies and Management, 24*(4), 520-549.

Klinger, D.A. (2004). Environment and Organization: Reviving a Perspective on the Police. *The Annals of the American Academy of Political and Social Science, 593*, 119-136.

Kohlberg, L. (1984). *The psychology of moral development: The nature and validity of moral sages*. New York, NY: Harper & Row.

Kraska, P.B., & Kappeler, V.E. (1997). Militarizing American Police: The Rise and Normalization of Paramilitary Units. *Social Problems, 44*, 1-18.

Landale, J. (2023, Oct. 18). Sudan conflict: Ethnic cleansing committed in Darfur, UK says. *BBC*. https://www.bbc.com/news/world-67020154

Law Enforcement Management Administrative Statistics (LEMAS). (2000). Department of Justice. Bureau of Justice Statistics.

Lewis, C. (1991). *The Ethics Challenge in Public Service*. (ed.). San Francisco: Jossey-Bass, Inc.

Lipsky, M. (1980). *Street-Level Bureaucracy: Dilemmas of the Individual in Public Services*. (ed.). New York: Russell Sage Foundation.

Lundman, R.J. (1980). *Police Behavior*. (ed.). New York: Oxford University Press.

Mastrofski, S.D., & Ritti, R.R. (1996). Police Training and the Effects of Organization on Drunk Driving Enforcement. *Justice Quarterly, 13*(2), 291-320.

Maynard-Moody, S., & Musheno, M. (2000). State Agent or Citizen Agent: Two Narratives of Discretion. *Journal of Public Administration Research and Theory, 10*(3), 329-358.

Paoline III, E.A. (2001). *Rethinking Police Culture: Officers' Occupational Attitudes*. (ed.). New York: LFB Scholarly Publishing LLC.

Quinn, R.E. (1984). *Applying the Competing Values Approach to Leadership*. New York: Pergamon Press.

Quinn, R.E. & Hall, R.H. (1983). *Environments, Organizations, and Policymakers: Toward an Integrative Framework*. Beverly Hills: Sage Publications, Inc.

Quinn, R.E., & Rohrbaugh, J. (1981). A Competing Values Approach to Organizational Effectiveness. *Public Productivity Review, 5*, 122-140.

Simon, R. (1995). Control in an Age of Empowerment. *Harvard Business Review, 73*(2), 80-88.

Slovak, J.S. (1988). Styles of Urban Policing: Organization, Environment, and Police Styles in Selected American Cities. (ed.). New York: New York University Press.

Van Wart, M. (1998). *Changing Public Sector Values*. (Ed.). New York: Garland Publishing, Inc.

Weber, D.C. (1999, August 26). *Warrior Cops: The Ominous Growth of Paramilitarism in American Police Departments*. CATO Institute.

Wilson, J.Q. (1989). *Bureaucracy: What Government Agencies Do and Why They Do It*. (ed.). New York: Basic Books.

Chapter 5
Justice

Chapter Objectives

1. Define the various concepts of justice within the justice system.
2. Apply concepts of justice to ethical dilemmas that commonly occur within the justice system.
3. Demonstrate a working knowledge of how each of the concepts of justice are connected to one another.

Introduction

When Daniel Penny put Jordan Neely in a chokehold on the New York City subway, he believed he was protecting his fellow citizens riding the subway that day. Neely died because of being placed in the chokehold and Penny was later arrested and then charged with second-degree manslaughter (Cramer et al., 2023). At the heart of this tragic event are questions regarding whether Penny was a good Samaritan protecting his fellow transit riders that day, whether Neely was an innocent victim, and what duties the riders had to intervene during the altercation.

The answers to these questions raised in the Penny case tell us whether a crime was committed and whether justice will be done. This chapter focuses on the concept of justice and several subcategories of justice. We begin with some background on studying crime and justice followed by considering definitions of justice, distributive justice, procedural justice, restorative justice, social justice, environmental justice, and the chapter ends by exploring a new concept - collaborative justice.

Justice Studies

August Vollmer is largely credited with creating the first criminal justice program at Berkeley in 1916. More recently, many programs have begun changing their names to Justice Studies as a way of placing the focus on the concept of justice within the system rather than a focus on crime that labels the individuals caught up in the system as criminals. **Justice studies** programs typically include courses on criminology, criminal law and procedure, policy, policing, courts, and corrections. Some disciplines outside of **justice studies** also include justice studies-type courses like philosophy, political science, history, sociology, psychology, and social work.

These connections between **justice studies** and other disciplines reflect the collaborative nature of the justice system. As **justice studies** is a relatively new field in comparison to other academic fields like psychology and the sciences, there are questions around what courses should be covered within these evolving programs. Some academic disciplines focus on sociological and criminological theories while others focus on systems of justice. Prior to the emergence of these programs, individuals who sought careers in the justice system had no formal academic background in their discipline before entering the workforce which begs the question how do we best prepare street-level bureaucrats for a life-long career in policing, courts, and/or corrections?

Furthermore, is an associate degree sufficient for entering a career in the system or do you need a bachelor's degree? A multitude of master's programs have also cropped up over the last several decades ranging across a broad spectrum including traditional sociological criminology programs, security studies, homeland security, justice systems, justice studies, immigration, cybersecurity, and comparative justice systems, just to name a few. Public administration programs also house several concentrations that focus on these fields in addition to preparing students for working in government leadership or not-for-profit fields.

Justice

Defining **justice** is more than simply considering justice and criminal laws; it is also concerned with human behavior and philosophy. The notion of justice relies heavily on the preferences, practices, and values within each culture in a very ethnocentric way. What is considered a crime in one culture may not be considered criminal in another. Even within the United States, there are conflicts of laws. Many states and the federal government criminalize marijuana possession and Nevada is the only state that has legalized prostitution. We tend to engage in normative thinking and operate within the confines of our own values, norms, experiences, and perspectives when defining notions of crime and justice. And the majority or dominant viewpoint is not the same as "**justice**", changing and morphing over time as society's values and perspectives continue to evolve. For example, the legalization of abortion with *Roe v. Wade* in 1973 was a major shift in women's healthcare only to be overturned by the *Dobbs* decision in 2022.

Justice can't be captured by any one viewpoint; it is complex, dynamic, and multidisciplinary. According to Aristotle, justice consists of righteousness, complete virtue, character, attitudes, and good habits. Aristotle's view establishes the building blocks for most definitions of justice which typically include four principles – fairness, equity, virtue, and consequences. Meanwhile, John Rawls (1971, p. 11) recognized that "In justice as fairness the original position of equality corresponds to the state of nature in the traditional theory of the social contract." According to Rawls (1971) then, justice is centered around the notion of fairness through equity often achieved through social contracts.

Fairness

Children learn what **fairness** means at an early age - equal shares for all (Wittig et al., 2013). **Fairness**, however, is more complex and there are multiple measures for **fairness** depending on whether the focus is on distribution of goods or **distributive fairness** versus how an individual is treated within a process or **procedural fairness** (Colquitt & Rodell, 2015). These concepts of **distributive** and **procedural fairness** are synonymous with the concepts of **distributive** and **procedural justice**. Rawls (1971) believed strongly that we are stronger as a society when we come together and help one another out. This can create conflict, however, when the fruits of our collective action need to be divided up.

> There is a conflict of interests since persons are not indifferent as to how the greater benefits produced by their collaboration are distributed, for in order to pursue their ends they each prefer a larger to a lesser share. A set of principles is required for choosing among the various social arrangements which determine this division of advantages and for underwriting an agreement on the proper distributive shares. These principles are the principles of social justice: they provide a way of assigning rights and duties in the basic institutions of society, and they define the appropriate distribution of the benefits and burdens of social cooperation. (Rawls, 1971, p. 4)

The focus of **distributive justice** is what measurement should be used to allocate society's resources. Distributing society's resources is not done equally or we would all have the same level of access to resources. Society values hard work, effort, and education which is rewarded with increased financial gain. But not everyone is able to work, to attain high levels of education, to expend efforts necessary to achieve increased financial gain which then begs the question what factors should determine how resources are distributed within society?

Egalitarian theories posit that distribution of society's resources should ensure equality of shares while Marxist theory focuses on the needs of those receiving the resource. Libertarians are more concerned with whether the government is determining who and how resources are distributed with an emphasis on less government involvement in these decisions while Utilitarians are interested in maximizing benefits for all of society. John Rawls believed in combining the utilitarian approach with a somewhat Marxist approach of benefiting those most in need and essentially ignoring a person's position in society otherwise (Pollock, 2021).

Case 5.1: Distributive Justice
Equal pay is a common example of a distributive justice issue in society. Within the justice system, an issue arises when considering what to pay incarcerated individuals for their work inside correctional facilities. These jobs are typically paid at rates far below any kind of minimum wage found in society for similar jobs. What would Rawls say about paying incarcerated individuals low wages? How would Marx respond to this type of treatment for incarcerated individuals?

The focus of **procedural justice** is fair treatment and fair processes afforded to the accused and victims while involved with the justice system. Research in both domestic violence and drunk driving cases indicates that people who feel they are treated fairly while being processed through the justice system are more likely to show up for court dates and less likely to recidivate as compared to individuals receiving punishment consistent with deterrence models (Paternoster et al., 1997; Tyler, 2007). People generally perceive that they are experiencing **procedural fairness/justice** when they are treated with respect, have a voice in decision-making, and trust the decision-maker (Tyler, 2004).

Case 5.2: Procedural Justice
The law does not require law enforcement officers to tell someone they've pulled over that they have the right to refuse a search of their car. Is this fair? Why or why not? What impact do you think having to tell people they can refuse would have on an officer's ability to search without probable cause?

Equity

The Equal Protection Clause is found within the Fourteenth Amendment to the U.S. Constitution and provides protections against discrimination or unequal treatment under the law based on race, ethnicity, and gender. **Equity** has become synonymous with inclusion in society. Attempts to rectify past discrimination using affirmative action programs in employment and education have been challenged by the U.S. Supreme Court (*Regents Univ. of California v. Bakke,* 1978) and continue to be challenged (*Students for Fair Admissions, Inc. (SFAI) v. President and Fellows of Harvard,* 2023). Has affirmative action balanced employment and education disparities such that we don't need to worry about discrimination and equal access in society?

Rawls (1971) believed that to achieve equity, we must agree on some basic principles to live in a fair society. To agree on these principles, we must approach our acceptance of them behind a **veil of ignorance** abandoning all biases and distinctions of social class and/or status.

> The principles of justice are chosen behind a veil of ignorance. This ensures that no one is advantaged or disadvantaged in the choice of principles by the outcome of natural chance or the contingency of social circumstances. Since all are similarly situated and no one is able to design principles to favor his particular condition, the principles of justice are the result of a fair agreement or bargain. (Rawls, 1971, p.11)

Achieving this pure state of ignorance has its challenges. Most people bring their personal biases to decision-making, but it certainly does have an effect on whether equity is achieved.

Virtue

Virtue Ethics is one of the oldest systems of ethics stressing development of character traits during early childhood that are considered good habits and avoiding bad character traits. Aristotle's vision of moral righteousness is what we consider to be a **virtue** today. What is **virtue** and what makes a person virtuous? Aristotle and Plato were keenly interested in these questions and focused on character traits to define **virtue**. According to Plato, **virtues** include wisdom, courage, temperance, and justice. A person who is knowledgeable, kind, sensitive, altruistic, attentive, and gentle relying on each of these traits working in tandem with one another could be considered virtuous (McDowell, 1979). Do I need to possess all these traits to be considered virtuous? Must I act virtuously all the time to be considered virtuous? Which character traits do you think we're missing from our lists?

Consequences

The **consequences** or response to immoral and/or illegal behavior can be formal or informal, but society tends to think of formal punishment as the natural response to such behavior. Theories of punishment vary from very punitive – retribution – to therapeutic – rehabilitation and restorative justice. Historically, punishment has been unfair, inequitable, and harsh. However, society still desires some type of **consequence** in response to immoral and/or illegal behavior. Do the **consequences** need to be punitive or simply the natural result of the behavior in question? Who should decide which **consequence** is appropriate in response to immoral and/or illegal behavior?

Case 5.3: Justice and consequences
Bail reform measures designed to promote decarceration release individuals on their own recognizance rather than forcing them to pay bail or remain incarcerated pending the outcome of their case for non-violent offenses. Critiques of this approach are concerned that without some type of consequence individuals will simply return to committing crimes. Are you in favor of bail reform? Why or why not?

Restorative Justice

Restorative justice (RJ) has emerged as a theory of punishment that revolves around the restoration of a victim after a crime or injustice has been committed against them and is further applied to the offender, as well as the community. According to Braithwaite (1998):

> Restorative justice is a process whereby all the parties with a stake in a particular offence come together to resolve collectively how to deal with the aftermath of the offence and its implications for the future. (p. 5)

The main elements of **RJ** include the parties participating voluntarily in an open and honest face-to-face encounter (Llewellyn & Howse, 1998). It is a marked departure from traditional punishment models where a judge or jury determines sanctions. **RJ** has connections to other theories of punishment including retribution theory where those who commit crimes should be punished based on the severity of the crime relying on the practice of just deserts. Similarly, offenders within a **RJ** model are either incarcerated/participating in community corrections or will receive some form of consequences for their behavior.

Other theories of punishment are connected to **RJ** like deterrence theory in that some studies show success with **RJ** models in terms of preventing future crime through punishment. Not all RJ models are linked to the sentencing process but focus more on restoring victims post-sentencing (see Case 5.4). Incapacitation, preventing crime by detaining wrongdoers in prison and separating them from the community, has either already occurred or may occur in a sentencing RJ model. Rehabilitation, a punishment theory that provides offenders the resources they need to battle addiction and significant mental health challenges, is often used in tandem with **RJ** practices.

Case 5.4: Restorative justice as a victim-centered approach
Laura is grieving the loss of her daughter, Anne, who was murdered by a stranger two years ago. The offender, Sam, was arrested, pleaded guilty and is serving a lengthy sentence for Anne's murder. As there wasn't a trial, Laura only had limited information surrounding Anne's death and while Laura has at least some closure in her daughter's case, Laura feels she needs to know more. Through a community RJ program, Laura has decided to meet with Sam and find out more about Anne's death. Would you want to meet with a loved one's murderer under similar circumstances? Why or why not? If you did, what would you want to ask the offender? What would you hope to discover?

Criminology has mostly focused on the offender and only in the past decade has there been a focus on the victim. Victimology has emerged as a field of study focusing on relationships between victims and offenders and the interactions between the victims and the justice system. The risks of victimization are best explained by routine activities theory which posits that criminal acts require a likely offender, a suitable target, and the absence of a capable guardian to protect the potential victim. Oftentimes there is a distinct connection between the victim and the offender leading to repeat victimization.

The legal structure of **RJ** within the justice system as an alternative sentencing model involves offenders being diverted from the traditional court process and can be used as a pre-sentence advisory component by judges, a condition of sentencing, a community correctional sentence, or a post-sentence component of pre-prison release. To participate in an **RJ** sentencing process, the offender must admit responsibility and meet face-to-face with the victim. As an alternative sentencing process, **RJ** is less formal than the traditional court processes, not requiring swearing in of participants and no formal record kept. It does, however, hold offenders accountable while giving victims a voice in the process with the goal of achieving reconciliation if possible.

RJ practices include an array of options that fall under several categories of processes. Circles and conferences offer mediation type alternative dispute resolution approaches which can be used in justice settings, but also as tools for generally resolving conflict outside the justice system as is the case on many college campuses (see Case 5.5). Within the options for circles there are both sentencing circles and circles of support and accountability. Circles can involve many people including victim(s), offender(s), and other impacted persons. A structured dialogue between the members of the circle is used for community-building or a discussion of difficult issues.

Conferences include restorative conferences, family group conferences, and victim offender dialogue. Conferences can also include a fairly large number of participants involving a structured and facilitated conversation between the victim and the offender with support from friends/advocates, counselors, social workers, and sometimes community members. The parties directly impacted by the conflict come to an agreement as to what will repair the harm and potentially rebuild trust between and among them.

Case 5.5: Restorative justice on college campuses
John and Noah are college first year students living on campus as roommates and sharing a common area with several other students within their dorm. During the first several months of school, John and Noah frequently invite new friends from other dorms to join them in the common room, staying up late, listening to loud music, cooking in the small kitchen area, and leaving behind their trash without cleaning up the next day. Not all students living in the dorm enjoy these late-night parties and have been complaining to the resident advisors and supervisors as the parties continue to escalate. Despite several warnings, John and Noah have only gotten worse, causing some minor damage to some of the furniture in the common area, and leaving an empty bong behind along with their textbooks on the kitchen table. Is a RJ process appropriate for resolving this dispute and if so, which might be more appropriate – a circle or a conference? Who would be appropriate for including in a RJ process designed to resolve John and Noah's unwelcome behavior? If you were a student living in this dorm, how would you want this resolved? or a student who attended one of the parties with John and Noah? How would you feel as the resident advisor and/or supervisor handling this dispute?

Both circles and conferences are guided by a trained facilitator who will educate everyone on the process, oversee pre-conference preparation, facilitate the conference, monitor post-conference, and provide mentoring (Orcutt et al., 2020). There are benefits of **RJ** over traditional court adjudication in giving victims a voice within the process that often gets lost in a traditional court process where the prosecutor, the judge, and the jury hold ultimate control over the outcome. Victims and other impacted individuals get to meaningfully participate in a process where the offender has to take responsibility for what they've done rather than deny culpability. The process being less formal makes for better communication in a flexible environment not constrained by legal rules of procedure. As a result, victims can feel validated, and relationships can be repaired when appropriate.

There are some issues that arise when relying on **RJ** over traditional court adjudication. Offenders can possibly manipulate the process to receive lesser sentences. Victims can be pressured into choosing **RJ** as a quicker resolution process when more traditional court may be appropriate particularly where a harsher sentence may be called for as is the case in, for example, sexual assault. Keeping victims safe in sexual assault cases could also be particularly challenging without the power of a court and/or correctional system controlling the outcome. The community also is given a voice in a process that elevates their role in ways that could be harmful to the victim and/or the offender where a community member may have mixed loyalties to the parties involved or may have a personal agenda that is not congruent with the case being addressed by **RJ**. Some cases may not be appropriate for **RJ** including those cases that involve the use of a weapon, where a victim has sustained physical injury, repeat offenders, minors, and special employment or student/teacher relationships between the victim and offender.

Despite the concerns over relying on **RJ** to resolve sexual assault cases, there is a movement both on college campuses and in society to shift from the traditional court model to a **RJ** model. According to Daly (2006), youth offenders who participated in **RJ** conferences for sexual assault charges had a lower reoffending rate than youth who went through the traditional court process. Youth who participated in counseling programs saw the biggest reductions in reoffending while threatening increased punishment had the opposite effect. **RJ** programs generally see significantly reduced recidivism rates across the board as compared to other approaches (Latimer et al., 2005).

Social Justice

Most people think of social justice as a mechanism for combatting injustices within society. Concepts already discussed in this chapter including fairness and equity are at the heart of social justice movements aimed at protecting marginalized communities. While many definitions for **social justice** exist, for the purposes of this discussion, **social justice** is:

> A fundamental valuing of fairness and equity in resources, rights and treatment for marginalized individuals and groups of people who do not share equal power in society because of their immigration, racial, ethnic, age, socioeconomic, religious heritage, physical ability, or sexual orientation status groups. (Constantine et al., 2007, p. 24)

Social justice can also be thought of in terms of what we owe society, what we owe one another, and how we determine the fair and equitable distribution of society's resources (Finn, 2020).

Social justice inequities occur wherever discrimination occurs throughout society. **Social injustice** acts as a type of social control particularly where individuals engage in deviant behavior as seen in the justice system (Reisch, 2013). The war on drugs is an example of using the justice system as a means of social control to perpetuate unjust outcomes on marginalized communities (Alexander, 2020). Consider how the law and its application by law enforcement and the courts has contributed to creating a racial caste system in the United States with respect to the war on drugs. Officers have discretion with respect to stop-and-frisk policies which disproportionally stop persons of color, legislatures pass laws that impose mandatory minimum sentences for non-violent drug crimes, and courts continue to sentence defendants disparately.

Case 5.6: Social justice activism
The Black Lives Matter movement protesting police brutality beginning in 2013, as well as the Occupy Wall Street movement protesting economic inequality beginning in 2011 rely on social disruption and civil disobedience to effect policy change. When is civil disobedience warranted in a civilly obedient society? Was Colin Kaepernick justified in taking a knee?

Environmental Justice

Protecting the environment is a social justice movement that has implications both outside and within the justice system. What aspects of **environmental justice** have implications within our justice system? Environmental crimes can occur when organizations wanting to save money in manufacturing their goods choose to ignore regulations designed to protect the environment. Illegal marijuana grows and moonshine distilleries also typically produce harm to the environment. Globally, trading wildlife and timber is also illegal and costs billions of dollars every year (UNEP, 2014). Organized crime also relies on pollution crime as a way to sell waste products like disposed tires, as well as a mechanism for money laundering (Interpol, 2022).

Collaborative Justice

During my lifetime, the justice system has morphed from a harshly punitive system to a distinctively more rehabilitative one. We've seen mass movements towards restorative justice and rehabilitation with the focus shifting from retribution to supporting victims and changing offender behavior. The justice system continually increases its reliance on various approaches that focus on collaboration both internal and external to the system. Some of these connections rely heavily on the civil law system and alternative dispute resolution (ADR). These collaborations bring police, courts, and corrections together partnering with social workers, psychologists, and community members primarily.

This chapter has focused on various concepts of justice, but it hasn't addressed collaboration and the role it plays in the justice system. **Collaboration** includes "mutually beneficial relationships between two or more parties who work together toward common goals by sharing responsibility, authority, and accountability for achieving results" (Chrislip & Larson, 1994, p. 5). Within business management, collaborations are valued as ways to improve decision making, working relationships, worker satisfaction, effective project implementation, and commitment to implementing results. Each of these improvements combined yields more effective outcomes.

Business leaders work hard at facilitating what is referred to as a **culture of collaboration** where employees "share a set of values and assumptions congruent with **collaboration** and generate behaviors and structures that embody the values and assumptions" (Schuman, 2006, p. 282). Developing a **culture of collaboration** requires building teams and communities through enhanced communication which fosters trust, meaning, purpose, and a sense of fairness and justice within work environments.

Given the many benefits of **collaboration**, one would think that all organizations would require high levels of collaboration in decision-making, however, this is not the case. **Collaboration** can take longer, require more resources, and where there are personality conflicts can cause as many problems as it solves. There must be commitment from organizational leadership and shared acceptance of employees that collaboration is necessary to change a culture from non-collaborative to **collaborative**.

Transforming an organization from non-collaborative to **collaborative** requires changing how employees engage in conversations from exclusive to inclusive. This in turn requires changing how people interact with one another and requires employees to relinquish control over what they do and how they do it, replacing the need to control with a focus on learning. And employees must abandon any preconceived ideas of what the solutions should be with respect to the myriad of problems faced by their agency to find solutions and take advantage of the collaboration itself.

Some of the most well-known collaborative justice programs within law enforcement are collaborations with social workers to reimagine policing and transfer mental health calls for service away from law enforcement and divert them to trained mental health professionals. Psychologists and social workers have also worked together with law enforcement to develop crisis intervention training to deescalate rather than make arrests. Crisis stabilization centers have been developed in communities where local jails and hospitals are overwhelmed with mental health and addicted patients as safe havens for connecting/reconnecting individuals to mental health case workers and addiction related services.

Case 5.7: Social workers and law enforcement collaboration
Reimagining policing calls for redirecting calls for service away from law enforcement and over to trained social workers for mental health related crisis. The results have been dramatic in terms of fewer use of force complaints against police officers. Should calls for service from citizens experiencing mental health issues be diverted in this way? Why or why not?

Collaboration in the courts began when judges started diverting defendants from jails and prisons in the early 1990s and funneling them into social services for addiction rehabilitation, as well as mental health services. These programs referred to as diversion or treatment courts have grown exponentially since then to over 4,000 programs nationwide. There are a variety of court diversion programs, each with a particular focus including adult drug treatment courts, mental health diversion courts, co-occurring disorder courts, veteran's courts, DUI, family treatment courts, juvenile treatment courts, opioid, and most recently human trafficking courts (NDCRC, 2021). Other court **collaborations** involve working with mediators for alternative dispute resolution, which is typically a civil court phenomenon, but has gained some traction in the criminal courts to resolve smaller matters.

Within prisons, **collaboration** occurs with respect to programming provided to incarcerated individuals. One of the most well-known programs is the Bard Prison Initiative where prisons provide liberal arts college degrees to prisoners during their incarceration. This **collaboration** requires college professors and administrators to work closely with prison staff in bringing courses into correctional settings. Other programs include providing parenting education, vocational programs, nurseries for babies born to mothers who are incarcerated, and incarcerated individuals providing dog training for service dogs. While each program is very different, the goals are to reduce recidivism, prepare incarcerated individuals for their transition back to society, and reduce behavioral problems during incarceration.

Conclusion

The conviction of Derek Chauvin for the death of George Floyd and the subsequent convictions of the three officers who assisted Chauvin feel like the very definition of achieving justice – fairness, equity, virtue, and consequences. A closer look raises questions of whether the sentence/consequences were fair considering a man lost his life. Does the bringing of federal civil rights violations fully address issues of equity in this case? This chapter has addressed the concept of justice and its related subcategories. Whether justice is achieved ultimately is a question for society to determine.

Debate Topics for In-Class Discussion

1. Relying on Restorative Justice in cases involving violence and a victim
    a. *Pro* – the victim plays a larger role in the outcome of the case and the consequences for the defendant
    b. *Con* – safety concerns for the defendant not having access to the traditional court process and traditional sanctions
2. Collaborative Justice diversion of defendants to treatment in felony cases
    a. *Pro* – defendants facing longer sentences and possible incarceration who are rehabilitated essentially are a bigger return in terms of outcomes for society and the defendant who has changed their life from one of continual incarceration and recidivism to a productive, non-offending citizen
    b. *Con* – the risks posed to society if the defendant doesn't change their behavior while being diverted

Terms

Justice studies
Justice
Fairness
Distributive fairness
Procedural fairness
Distributive justice
Procedural justice
Equity
Veil of ignorance
Virtue Ethics
Virtue
Consequences
Restorative Justice (RJ)
Social Justice
Environmental Justice
Collaboration
Culture of Collaboration

References

Alexander, M. (2020). *The new Jim Crow: Mass incarceration in the age of colorblindness*. The New Press.

Braithwaite, J. (1998). Restorative justice. *The handbook of crime and punishment*, 323-344.

Chrislip, D. D., & Larson, C. E. (1994). *Collaborative leadership: How citizens and civic leaders can make a difference* (Vol. 24). Jossey-Bass.

Colquitt, J. A., & Rodell, J. B. (2015). Measuring justice and fairness.

Constantine MG, Hage SM, Kindaichi MM, et al. (2007) Social justice and multicultural issues: implications for the practice and training of counselors and counseling psychologists. Journal of Counseling and Development 85: 24–29.

Cramer, M., Meko, H., & Nierenberg, A. (2023). What We Know About Jordan Neely's Killing. New York Times (Online).

Daly, K. (2006). Restorative justice and sexual assault: An archival study of court and conference cases. *British Journal of Criminology, 46*(2), 334-356.

Dobbs v. Jackson Women's Health Organization, 597 U.S. ____ (2022). (1966, February 18). Finest of the Finest. *Time*.

Environmental crime. INTERPOL. (n.d.). https://www.interpol.int/en/Crimes/Environmental-crime

Finn, J. L. (2020). *Just practice: A social justice approach to social work.* Oxford University Press.

Latimer, J., Dowden, C., & Muise, D. (2005). The effectiveness of restorative justice practices: A meta-analysis. The prison journal, 85(2), 127-144.

Llewellyn, J. & Howse, R. (1998). Restorative justice: A conceptual framework. Ottawa: Law Commission of Canada.

McDowell, J. (1979). Virtue and reason. *The Monist, 62*(3), 331-350.

National Drug Court Resource Center (NDCRC). (2021). Interactive Maps.

Orcutt, M., Petrowski, P. M., Karp, D. R., & Draper, J. (2020). Restorative justice approaches to the informal resolution of student sexual misconduct. JC & UL, 45, 204.

Paternoster, R., Bachman, R., Brame, R., & Sherman, L. (1997). Do fair procedures matter? The effect of procedural justice on spouse assault. Law & Society Review, 31, 163–204.

Pollock, J. M. (2021). *Ethical dilemmas and decisions in criminal justice.* Cengage Learning.

Rawls, J. (1971). *A Theory of Justice,* 2nd Edition 1999, Cambridge, MA: Harvard University Press.

Regents of Univ. of California v. Bakke, 438 U.S. 265 (1978).

Reisch, M. (Ed.). (2013). *Social policy and social justice.* Sage Publications.

Report: Pollution crime is highly profitable, organized and harming the planet. (2022). Interpol.

Roe v. Wade, 410 U.S. 113 (1973).

Schuman, S. (Ed.). (2006). *Creating a culture of collaboration: The International Association of Facilitators handbook* (Vol. 4). John Wiley & Sons.

Students for Fair Admissions, Inc. (SFAI) v. President and Fellows of Harvard, 600 U.S. 181 (2023).

Tyler, T. R. (2004). Procedural justice. In A. Sarat (Ed.), The Blackwell companion to law and society. London, U.K.: Blackwell Publishing.

Tyler, T. R. (2007). Procedural justice and the courts. Court Review, 44, 26–31.

UNEP: Putting a stop to global environmental crime has become an imperative. (2014). *UN Chronicle, 51*(2), 8–10.

Wittig, M., Jensen, K., & Tomasello, M. (2013). Five-year-olds understand fair as equal in a mini-ultimatum game. *Journal of experimental child psychology, 116*(2), 324-337.

Chapter 6
Comparative and International Justice

Chapter Objectives

1. Define comparative criminology and its connection to ethics.
2. Recognize the various types of transnational crimes and the problems that arise in addressing them.
3. Identify ethical problems associated with terrorism and the global war on terror.

Introduction

In July 2023, Interpol captured the leader behind an international syndicate, known as OPERA1OR, that stole somewhere between $11 and $30 million dollars from banks and telecom companies in 15 different countries. Around the same time, the U.S. discovered that China had been hacking into confidential government emails. And since El Chapo's extradition for drug trafficking in 2017, his four sons have taken over his illegal drug trade focusing on the highly lethal synthetic fentanyl rather than cocaine. Each of these news stories are examples of transnational crime and the responses to those crimes pose unique moral dilemmas for the justice system.

This chapter now turns our focus away from the bases for studying morality and ethics within the criminal justice system and shifts our focus towards a global perspective regarding crime. We covered deviant behavior and delinquency briefly in Chapter 1 and this chapter builds off the theories explored therein. We begin by looking at different types of court systems, comparative criminology in terms of issues that arise when considering societies globally, and the societal factors that contribute to crime. We then consider various types of transnational crime and end with a discussion of terrorism and counter terrorism measures.

Adversarial, Inquisitorial, and Religious Court Systems

There are three main types of court systems in the world – common law systems, civil law systems, and systems that rely on religious doctrine. In a common law system, there are statutes that are interpreted by judges and the approach is adversarial where the attorneys control the presentation of evidence. For example, the United States relies on statutes, but is also heavily influenced by precedent and takes an adversarial approach making it a common law system. Civil law systems rely more on codes that are interpreted by legal experts where the role of the judge is to have more control over the investigation of a case as in **inquisitorial systems**. Religious legal systems rely on ecclesiastical leadership to determine the law and resolving disputes. Many religious legal systems are also hybrids of either common or civil law systems.

In the United States, the civil and criminal court systems are adversarial where the attorneys control the presenting of evidence and arguing the case before a judge or jury. The judge's role is to be objective as a moderator determining points of law. Both sides of the case are assumed to be on equal footing. The legal battle is similar to a contest with the lawyers controlling how the truth is presented to the decider of fact. Great Britain and Australia also have adversarial court systems as do many court systems that rely on common law or judge-made law. The court proceedings are tightly controlled by rules of procedure and evidence which can keep some evidence from being presented to the trier of fact (Newlyn, 2018).

Many European countries like Switzerland, Italy, France, Belgium, and the Netherlands rely on an **inquisitorial system** where the judge takes center stage in a role that appears much like a cross between judge and prosecutor. Rather than relying on common law, the inquisitorial courts rely on codified laws and do not have strict rules of procedure. As such, the judge is tasked with pursuing the truth of the case objectively and without worrying about rules like Hearsay that prevent some evidence from being made a part of the case. The inquisitorial process can be lengthy as a result, as the judge is expected to be thorough in pursuing the truth (Newlyn, 2018). For example, a case has to go through many steps to get to the point where it is before the judge, and this can take a year or longer for a simple assault.

Case 6.1: Adversarial v. Inquisitorial
In 2007 an exchange student in Italy, Meredith Kercher, was murdered and her roommate, Amanda Knox, along with Amanda's boyfriend, Raffaele Sollecito, were wrongfully convicted of Meredith's murder. Italy has an inquisitorial court system, and their process received a lot of negative publicity as a result of mistakes made during the process. There is a documentary called Amanda Knox that highlights the investigation and court process. How important is the process itself towards achieving justice? Would you rather have a judge in charge of your investigation and trial (inquisitorial) or law enforcement and attorneys (adversarial)?

Comparative Criminology

Criminology is a commonly taught subject in most criminal justice studies programs. Figuring out why people commit crimes is central to understanding crime as a social phenomenon and as social behavior. Not all countries approach crime in the same way in terms of their respective attempts at maintaining social order and achieving justice. Studying crime across countries is challenging given that not all countries define, report, and record crime data in a similar way. Despite these challenges, some theories emerge regarding crime and the moral dilemmas of combating crime globally.

The Civilization Theory identifies a link between civilized society emerging and a decrease in violent crime. The idea is that as society became more civil it was transformed into a less violent more peaceful place. However, as society evolved this also led to several theories driving crime related to capitalism and industrialization. When industrial development occurs within a country, the social processes that accompany that development can lead to increased criminality. This theory essentially recognizes that while growth and modernization can have positive effects on society, it can also give rise to increases in opportunity to commit fraud, as well as violent crime, particularly where people come to live together in large urban cities (Durkheim, 2014). Another related theory of crime involves the disruption of indigenous cultures as a result of the expansion of capitalistic societies. The merging of these two very different cultures then creates class conflict and inequality. This is known as **World System Theory** and is based on Marxist theories of the exploitation of the indigenous culture (Neuman & Berger, 1988; Wallerstein, 1974).

There is a strong relationship between the theory of modernization and **Opportunity Theory** which posits that crime occurs as a result of modern economies and social organization giving those who would commit crimes increased opportunities to do so. Cohen and Felson (1979) further describe **Opportunity Theory** within the context of **Routine Activities Theory** which holds that where there is a likely target or victim and someone who is willing to commit the crime, then the crime will happen when those two elements converge simultaneously within an environment conducive to committing the crime.

A different approach to studying crime focuses on gender inequality and gender differences and is known as the **Feminist Theory**. Considering that criminological theories of crime focus on male experiences, Feminist Theory provides a mechanism for considering the impact of gender differences in crime rates, women as victims of crime, women as participants of crime, and differences in the rates of gendered crimes (Simpson, 1989).

Case 6.1: Modernization
In some areas of Mexico and Latin America psychedelic plants can be harvested and studied for the development of new medicines. Extracting these plants is problematic in that they grow on land occupied by indigenous communities who may not be willing to share the plants and what they know about the use of the plants. How should researchers approach extracting the plants? What considerations are there and who should profit from any future pharmaceuticals developed from the plants? What if the indigenous communities refuse to allow researchers access to plants with the potential of saving lives? If researchers are allowed to harvest the plants and learn from the indigenous people, what impact might this new relationship and ongoing interaction have on their culture?

Transnational Crime

There are a variety of crimes that cross borders. **Transnational crimes** typically are motivated by financial gain committed by organized criminal syndicates. Tracking and capturing perpetrators of transnational crime requires concerted efforts of multiple countries, not just those whose citizens are victims of the crimes perpetrated, but also the countries where the perpetrators may be working and/or hiding. We will focus on some of the most common types of transnational crime which include cybercrime, corruption, trafficking, and terrorism.

Cybercrime

Cybercrime occurs where computers and cellphones are linked to criminal activity generally in cyber-attacks, cyber theft, and other security incidents like surveillance and spyware. In a **cyber-attack**, the computer systems themselves are the target of the criminal act whereas in other security incidents the target is typically acquiring confidential or private information. With **cyber theft**, the computer is merely a tool used to commit the crime of stealing. Because computers are at the heart of these types of crime, there are a host of ethical issues that arise when deciding how to approach preventing and thwarting cybercrime.

For example, cellphones pit two cherished values of rights to privacy and protecting citizens' safety against one another. In an epic battle between cellphone manufacturers like Apple and law enforcement agencies like the FBI, the issue is whether we allow intelligence gathering agencies and law enforcement the right to have access to encrypted data from our phones. Apple argues that they do not have access themselves to a backdoor that would allow access to cellphone user privately encrypted data. The FBI meanwhile argues that they need to be able to get access to private information while investigating crimes to prevent potentially catastrophic terrorist attacks and to track down serial killers. These moral dilemmas are not exclusive to any one country considering over 86% of the world's population own smartphones (Laricchia, 2023).

Malware, spyware, phishing scams, and **cyber theft** present problems of finding and capturing perpetrators of these crimes who can live anywhere in the world and attack everywhere indiscriminately. Consider the case of the syndicate OPERA1OR stealing from 15 different countries. Once found, which country will prosecute first? The country that has the strongest case may be the logical solution but may not be the country that captures OPERA1OR's leader and/or may not be the country where the leader is found. If OPERA1OR's leader is found, what of the other members of the syndicate? They could continue, perhaps evade **extradition** – the process of transferring a captured criminal suspect from one jurisdiction to another to face their criminal charges - depending on which country they reside in and whether that country has **extradition** agreements with the countries seeking their capture.

Corruption

Within the context of transnational crime, **corruption** here includes the abuse of entrusted power typically perpetrated by someone within a government or authoritative agency for private gain. Corruption undermines political, social, and economic stability within a country.

Corruption contributes to global crime since transnational criminals are aided by the complicity of corrupt public officials. **Corruption** includes bribery, embezzlement of public funds, influencing trade, and concealment of **corruption** proceeds.

Sam Bankman-Fried is a prime example of **corruption**. His cryptocurrency hedge fund, Alameda Research, paid millions to the Chinese government in bribes to unfreeze their accounts there. Once their accounts were unfrozen, the hedge fund continued to engage in more illegal activity by trading on behalf of their customers in a fraudulent scheme (Sigalos & Goswami, 2023). U.S. companies bribing officials in other countries in order to do business there may be allowed or considered expected within those countries receiving the economic benefits of the bribery funds, but it is illegal for U.S. companies to do so under the Foreign Corrupt Practices Act.

Case 6.2: Influencing U.S. Elections
Yevgeny Prigozhin, the former leader of the Wagner Group military forces used in Russia's war against Ukraine, openly admitted to using social media in an effort to undermine U.S. elections. The goal was to influence public opinion in the 2016 presidential campaign. Prigozhin had been a longtime friend of Russian President Vladimir Putin. What are the implications for any political candidate who might benefit from this outside influence? Can this kind of activity be regulated and/or controlled? Does it matter whether Artificial Intelligence is spreading disinformation as opposed to an individual at a computer screen?

Case 6.3: Iraq
After the 2003 Iraqi war, America pledged to help Iraq rebuild its infrastructure and train its police forces to provide stability and keep insurgents from reclaiming the country. Widespread corruption over an eight-year period and seeing no end in sight, the U.S. withdrew from Iraq. Similarly, the U.S. withdrew from Afghanistan in 2020 and in both situations, the results were disastrous. In the war on terror, the U.S. and other countries are fighting insurgents rather than in a traditional war where the fight is between recognized countries. What duties do countries owe one another to fight internal corruption, provide stability, and promote democracy globally? What costs should citizens be willing to pay in order to live up to these duties?

Drug Trafficking

While the prevalence of one drug over another has changed, **drug trafficking** has otherwise remained constant. According to the United Nations Office on Drugs and Crime (UNODC, 2023), almost 6% of the world's population has used drugs over the last 12 months. While cannabis is the most widely used drug, millions of people still turn to opiates like heroin, amphetamines, cocaine, ecstasy-type substances, and non-medical use of pharmaceuticals. Opiates are the deadliest in terms of fatal overdoses largely attributed to the introduction of synthetic opioid drugs like fentanyl. Drug addiction comes at a high cost to those who are addicted causing them to lose their family, friends, jobs, and homes.

A strong painkiller approved by the Food and Drug Administration (FDA), Fentanyl is a leading cause of drug overdoses. In Canada alone in 2021, almost 70,000 people overdosed on opiates with fentanyl while in the U.S. that number exceeded 70,000 within the same year (UNODC, 2023; NIH, 2023). Overdose deaths have risen so dramatically globally, partly attributed to the stresses of the pandemic, that there has been a push to make NARCAN kits and training more widely available. NARCAN is an over-the-counter nasal spray that immediately reverses the effects of an overdose while in progress. One complaint that law enforcement have with using NARCAN is that as soon as they revive someone, that person goes right back to using again without any kind of mechanism for connecting them with immediate treatment.

President Nixon famously declared a **War on Drugs** in 1971 calling drug addiction a public enemy and passing laws aimed at reducing the availability and use of illegal drugs in the United States. The **War on Drugs** is considered a global conflict requiring cooperation with countries like Mexico, Nicaragua, Honduras, and Columbia who become suppliers of illegal narcotics. Fighting the **War on Drugs** has cost the U.S. federal and state governments billions of dollars annually, not to mention the human costs of mass incarceration. The **War on Drugs** has been particularly harsh on the poor and people of color. It has also economically hurt farmers who cultivate coca plants for legitimate purposes within their own countries as they become targets for drug interdiction campaigns.

Drug trafficking often involves other illegal activities like the illegal trafficking of firearms. From 2009 to 2011, the Bureau of Alcohol, Firearms, Tobacco, and Explosives (ATF) ran an operation called Fast and Furious to track illegal gun running amongst Mexican drug cartels. It is estimated that the ATF lost track of about 1,400 of the guns they were tracking with this operation and several of those lost guns ended up at a crime scene where a Border Patrol agent was murdered. After an investigation into the Fast and Furious program, 14 employees of the ATF and the Department of Justice (DOJ) were found to be responsible for the lost guns through mismanagement.

Case 6.4: The War on Drugs
Is it time to end the War on Drugs? Can the government declare drug addiction a public health emergency rather than something the criminal justice system must solve? What would the problems be with making this kind of transition with respect to drug addiction from a punitive approach to a harm reduction, medical health type approach?

Human Trafficking

There are two types of **human trafficking** which include **labor trafficking** and **sex trafficking**. According to U.S. anti-**human trafficking** policy, anyone who uses force, fraud, or coercion to control another person for labor or sexual activity is committing a crime. One problem with tracking the prevalence of **human trafficking** is that not every country relies on the same definition. Some countries and researches only consider **sex trafficking** to be **human trafficking** even though **labor trafficking** is much more widespread. Others do not consider that men are capable of being trafficked and only count women and children who are being trafficked. And countries sharing this kind of data do so voluntarily resulting in many countries who refuse to share data regarding **human trafficking**.

Identifying when and where **human trafficking** is happening, tracking those who are being trafficked, measuring all the details of trafficking, and capturing those who are perpetrating **human trafficking** is nearly impossible. Typically, a **human trafficking** ring is broken up when a series of crimes are discovered that may not seem connected to human trafficking like prostitution, drug possession and/or distribution, assaults, and child labor. It is generally up to local law enforcement to figure out whether **human trafficking** is occurring with respect to what may seem on the surface to be garden-variety crimes.

A bigger problem is figuring out what to do with the victims of **human trafficking**. Since many are engaging in criminal activity once they've been coerced into their unfortunate circumstances, does this mean they are complicit in committing a crime? As mentioned, some very serious crimes may have been committed including murder. Showing coercion in a court of law can be challenging. Additionally, once captured, victims find themselves outside their home country creating the dilemma of whether to return the victim to the home they fled.

Terrorism

Defining **terrorism** can vary greatly. Most definitions focus on politically motivated violence designed to intimidate the public. For example, in the United States, terrorism is defined as:

> . . . the premeditated, politically motivated violence perpetrated against noncombatant targets by subnational groups or clandestine agents. (U.S. Code, 2023)

The Global Terrorism Database (GTD) first created in 2002 defines **terrorism** as:

> Acts by non-state actors involving threatened or actual use of illegal force or violence to attain a political, economic, religious, or social goal through fear, coercion, or intimidation. (START, 2023)

Meanwhile, the U.S. State Department defines **terrorism** as:

> . . . activity that (1) involves a violent act or an act dangerous to human life, property, or infrastructure; and (2) appears to be intended to intimidate or coerce a civilian population; to influence the policy of a government by intimidation or coercion; or to affect the conduct of a government by mass destruction, assassination, kidnapping, or hostage-taking. (U.S. State Department, 2023)

Violence is used as a tool to instill fear and coerce either governments or society in aiding the terrorist group to achieve their goals. Terrorist groups are motivated by ideological belief systems that are religious or political or some combination of both. While **terrorism** can be international or domestic in scope, this chapter focuses on international **terrorism**.

According to the GTD (START, 2023), in 2020 Afghanistan remains the frontrunner in terms of total number of terrorist attacks and deaths accounting for almost a third of all terrorist attacks and almost half of deaths from **terrorism** globally. Iraq comes in second in terms of terrorist attacks but is a significantly distant second making up approximately 9% of attacks with only a fraction of deaths from terrorist events as compared to Afghanistan. While not experiencing as many attacks as other countries, several saw significant deaths as a result of terrorist activity including Nigeria, the Democratic Republic of the Congo, and Ethiopia (see Table 1).

Country	Attacks	Attacks %	Deaths
Afghanistan	2,604	31%	10,081
Iraq	764	9%	525
Nigeria	478	6%	2,102
Yemen	474	6%	903
India	450	5%	212
Democratic Republic of the Congo	310	4%	1,356
Philippines	294	3%	280
Pakistan	294	3%	322
Somalia	280	3%	885
Syria	256	3%	973
Mozambique	220	3%	709
Mali	138	2%	566
Burkina Faso	110	1%	681
Ethiopia	53	1%	1,330
Worldwide	**8,438**		**22,847**

Table 6.1: *Terrorist Attacks by Locations 2020* START (2023)

There are several problems with measuring terrorist events particularly because there are so many definitions that identifying what constitutes a terrorist event can be challenging. Not all countries share data so much of terrorist-related crimes go unreported or are not publicly available for studying. Depending on ideology, one group may be labeled a terrorist organization by some and freedom fighters by others.

Case 6.5: Defining terrorism
In 2008, then President George W. Bush (Jr.) visited Britain and around 2,500 people showed up in London to protest his war policies (Tran, 2008). Bush faced controversy over his invasions of Afghanistan and Iraq post 9/11. His administration claimed that Iraq was buying uranium to make weapons of mass destruction. These claims later proved false, being based on faulty intelligence. Protesters carried signs calling Bush a terrorist. Was Bush a terrorist under any of the definitions we've explored?

Countering Transnational Crime

The **International Criminal Police Organization**, **INTERPOL**, facilitates cross-border criminal police cooperation to combat transnational crime. It first came into existence post World War One and has evolved significantly since that time. It is considered a Non-Governmental Organization (NGO) since countries do not need to sign treaty agreements in order to join. It is in fact law enforcement organizations within a country or state who join **INTERPOL** rather than through an act of their governing body (Sheptycki, 2004).

Operating with dual headquarters in Lyon, France and Singapore, **INTERPOL** has satellite offices within its member countries. **INTERPOL** operates several crime databases and offers general investigative support to member countries. There are 195 members from a variety of countries, and they meet annually to consider policy and operational issues. Issues arise regarding mechanisms for holding **INTERPOL** accountable, not unlike holding law enforcement accountable within domestic contexts. This becomes particularly important when some member agencies request support from **INTERPOL** in finding dissidents and political opponents.

The **United Nations** (UN) operates much of its crime and justice work through the **Office on Drugs and Crime** (**UNODC**). Their mission includes global drug and **human trafficking**, various types of organized crime, corruption, and economic crimes, as well as **terrorism**. **UNODC**'s focus includes not only prevention, but also treatment for victims of **human trafficking**. Their headquarters is in Vienna, but they have approximately 130 offices worldwide. Funded by a variety of governments, they offer support in terms of advice and research to 146 member states.

Amnesty International has criticized **UNODC** for refusing to address countries that impose the death penalty for drug related crimes. According to Amnesty International (2023), more than a third of global executions are for drug-related offenses. Unfortunately, it's challenging to count executions as not all countries share information regarding who they have sentenced to death and the reason behind the sentence.

Created in 1997, the **Organisation for the Prohibition of Chemical Weapons** (**OPCW**) is tasked with promoting and verifying the elimination of chemical weapons by member states globally. The destruction of chemical weapons is important given the dangers inherent in their use, falling into the wrong hands, and devastating effects on the environment as they degrade over time. The use of chemical weapons is considered a war crime which falls under the jurisdiction of the **International Criminal Court (ICC)**. The **OPCW** has 193 member states and is closing in on 100% compliance from each.

Within the U.S., combatting transnational crime requires enhanced inspection, detection, and monitoring of borders. Most federal law enforcement agencies address transnational crime on some level. For example, Immigration and Customs Enforcement (ICE), Customs and Border Patrol, U.S. Coast Guard, Drug Enforcement Administration

(DEA), Central Intelligence Agency (CIA), Homeland Security Investigations (HSI) for the Department of Homeland Security (DHS), just to name a few. Many local and state law enforcement agencies also have specialized units addressing transnational crime. As a result, intergovernmental relationships between these agencies become critical as questions of who may have jurisdiction over a criminal enterprise arise.

Countering terrorism and terrorist groups is rather complicated, involving a variety of approaches and strategies including gathering intelligence, passing policies aimed at combatting terrorism, engaging in diplomacy, and relying on propaganda to influence members of terrorist groups. Military interventions are usually seen as a last resort tactic in the war on terror. Three strategies are controversial including the use of enhanced interrogation techniques in intelligence gathering which is discussed in Chapter 10, instigating attacks on governments that sponsor terrorism and terrorist groups which is also discussed in Chapter 10, and extraordinary rendition or extradition in capturing and returning terrorists to countries where they face criminal charges.

What happens when someone suspected of terrorist activity is located in a country outside of where the terrorist act they perpetrated occurred? The legal process is to arrest the suspect with cooperation from the local authorities and then request **extradition** from that country to the country where the suspect is wanted for the crime committed. **Extradition** is a process controlled by courts that forces a suspect to face the legal consequences of their action. Unfortunately, **extradition** is a long process that can result in the suspect being set free and not being extradited for a variety of reasons. For example, if the country that is requesting extradition of a suspect has a harsher punishment than allowed in the host country, then the host country will generally not allow **extradition**. This happens where the requesting country has the death penalty as a possible sanction while the host country does not.

Extraordinary rendition, also known simply as **rendition**, is an extralegal process that allows interrogation and removal of a suspect from the country where they've been located, the host country, to the country of the criminal offense. **Rendition** is an abduction in order to avoid the legal **extradition** process that can be lengthy and not always effective. Sometimes the host country is in agreement with the **rendition**, willing to look the other way and even help with the abduction, and sometimes the host country is not even aware the **rendition** is happening. The United Nations Convention against torture does not allow detainees abroad to be sent to a country where they will be tortured so if the **rendition** occurs and the suspect is being sent somewhere that sanctions torture, the **rendition** is in violation of humanitarian law.

Case 6.6: The Extraordinary Rendition of Abu Omar (#318 - Georgetown University's Diplomacy Case Studies)
In the case of Abu Omar, an Egyptian born cleric, several CIA officers aided in his rendition to Egypt. Omar was a known supporter of terrorist groups and someone who regularly recruited suicide bombers. He was also a former leader of an Islamic extremist group. Egypt is known to rely on torture within their justice system. When the Italian government found out that Omar had been abducted and returned to Egypt by CIA and Italian military intelligence officers, the Prime Minister requested the extradition of the CIA officers responsible for the rendition so they could face charges in Italy for conducting what the Italian government considered to be illegal operations. Should Italy have requested the extradition of the CIA officers involved in Omar's rendition? Why or why not? What are the consequences of this request? What are the consequences for the U.S. should they deny the request? and if the U.S. did extradite the CIA officers, what would the consequences be?

Conclusion

The top 11 transnational crime combined revenues worldwide range from $1.6 to $2.2 billion dollars on average annually (Kar and Spanjers, 2017). The toll that these crimes take on society is impossible to calculate and combatting these crimes is challenging requiring coordination across multiple jurisdictions worldwide. The UN, the International Criminal Court, and INTERPOL are just a few of the organizations dedicated to collaborating in combating transnational crime. Their power, however, is limited without cooperation from the countries that harbor transnational criminals.

Debate Topics for In-Class Discussion

1. Holding human trafficking victims accountable
    a. *Pro* – victims of human trafficking are often involved in criminal activity and must be held responsible for their illegal actions
    b. *Con* – victims of human trafficking should not be held responsible since they have been coerced into their criminal behavior
2. Engaging in extraordinary rendition practices
    a. *Pro* – rendition practices can be useful in preventing future terrorist events
    b. *Con* – rendition practices can violate humanitarian law, local laws and customs of host countries, and usurp traditional extradition law

Terms

Inquisitorial system
Criminology
Civilization Theory
World System Theory
Opportunity Theory
Routine Activities Theory
Feminist Theory
Transnational crime
Cybercrime
Cyber-attack
Cyber theft
Corruption
Drug trafficking
War on Drugs
Human trafficking
Labor trafficking
Sex trafficking
Terrorism
International Criminal Police Organization (INTERPOL)
United Nations Office on Drugs and Crime (UNODC)
Organisation for the Prohibition of Chemical Weapons (OPCW)
International Criminal Court (ICC)
Counter-terrorism
Extradition
Extraordinary rendition or rendition

References

Cohen, L. E., & Felson, M. (1979). Social change and crime rate trends: A routine activity approach. *American Sociological Review*, *44*, 588-608.

Death Sentences and Executions. Amnesty International Global Report. *Amnesty International.*

Durkheim, E. (2014). *The division of labor in society*. Simon and Schuster.

Kar, D., & Spanjers, J. (2017). Transnational crime and the developing world. *Global Financial Integrity*, 53-59.

Laricchia, F. (2023, September 28). *Smartphone penetration worldwide as share of global population 2016-2022*. Statista.

National Institute of Health (NIH). (2023). *Drug Overdose Death Rates*. National Institute on Drug Abuse.

Neuman, W.L. & Berger, R.J. (1988). Competing perspectives on cross-national crime: An evaluation of theory and evidence. *The Sociological Quarterly, 29*(2), 281–313.

Newlyn, D. (2018). Adversarial vs. Inquisitorial legal systems: Rousseau, truth, justice and God. International Journal of Research in Applied, Natural and Social Sciences, 6(5), 165-174.

Sheptycki, J. (2004). The accountability of transnational policing institutions: The strange case of Interpol. *Canadian Journal of Law and Society/La Revue Canadienne Droit et Société, 19*(1), 107-134.

Sigalos, M., & Goswami, R. (2023, Mar 28). Sam Bankman-Fried paid over $40 million to bribe at least one official in China, DOJ alleges in new indictment. *MSNBC*.

Simpson, S. S. (1989). Feminist theory, crime, and justice. *Criminology, 27*(4), 605-632.

START (National Consortium for the Study of Terrorism and Responses to Terrorism). (2022). Global Terrorism Database 1970 - 2020 [data file]. https://www.start.umd.edu/gtd

Tran, M. (2008, June 16). George Bush in Britain: Police investigate anti-war protests. *The Guardian*.

United Nations Office on Drugs and Crime (UNODC). (2023). *World Drug Report 2023*.

U.S. Code, Title 22, Chapter 38, §2656f[d] retrieved July 28, 2023.

Wallerstein, I.M. (1974). *The Modern World-System*. New York: Academic Press.

Chapter 7
Ethics in Policing

Chapter Objectives

1. Expose students to some of the causes of unethical behavior in policing.
2. Discuss the situational, organizational, and individual factors that influence police officer behavior.
3. Recognize the impact that the police officer's role in society has on their moral conduct. Explore the police culture within an organization.
4. Consider the ethical ramifications of police tactics utilized in investigations and interrogations.

Introduction

Spectacular scandals illustrate the underlying issue of the performance and accountability of public servants. The videotaped murder of George Floyd in Minnesota, the Rodney King beating in Los Angeles, the torture of a Haitian immigrant with a plunger in New York, as well as the widespread corruption in Los Angeles, New York, and New Orleans police forces are just a few of the examples found within law enforcement. When one officer commits a transgression, the entire agency suffers particularly when the news media reports the incident.

According to the Washington Post, over the last decade approximately 85,000 officers have been either investigated or disciplined in over 200,000 incidents (Kelly & Nichols, 2020). There are typically anywhere between 600,000 to over 800,000 sworn officers in state and local departments at any one time. The Bureau of Justice Statistics also reports that about 2% of the public who have police encounters self-report experiencing either the threat of force or the use of nonfatal force during the police contact (Tapp & Davis, 2022).

While excessive force garners the most attention in the media, this chapter explores a variety of ethical issues that arise for law enforcement. We begin with an exploration of why officers might commit unethical acts. This is followed by an exploration of the role of law enforcement in society. We also look at factors that influence officer attitudes and behavior and police culture. Finally, we will consider the ethics of relying on certain police tactics used in investigations and interrogations.

Reasons for Unethical Behavior

Steinberg and Austern (1990) summarize some of the **reasons why officers might commit unethical acts**. Some claim they did not realize it was against the law, policy or procedure. Some officers admit that unethical conduct can be the result of basic stupidity. There are those police officers who believe corruption is a part of the job, that it is required to survive their job, or that it is a game. Some of the most destructive reasons in history center around those who believe that they are doing the right thing (which is also known as **noble cause corruption)** going along with what the agency requires, or simply just following orders. Other officers admit it is a way to speed up the way the system processes clients, to help a friend, to abuse the system, to feed their ego, to satisfy their greedy nature, for personal gain, as a type of revenge, or to solve a financial problem (Steinberg & Austern, 1990).

Individuals respond in a variety of ways to inefficient and/or inferior working conditions. According to Hirschman (1970), employees who face undesirable work environments can exit the organization, voice their discontent, remain loyal to the organization and ignore the situation, or neglect their work as a passive aggressive response (Rusbult et al., 1982; Farrell, 1983; Withey & Cooper, 1989). Police officers may accept misconduct in their personal values as a passive aggressive response to undesirable working conditions. Officers may tolerate the misconduct of other officers and not report those officers out of loyalty. Some officers, however, may report the misconduct of fellow officers, an act more commonly called whistleblowing which was explored in Chapter 1 of this textbook.

Police officers, however, are not typically prone to reporting fellow officers for misconduct. The **code of silence** is well documented within the police culture literature (Klockars et al., 2004; Vila & Morris, 1999; Human Rights Watch, 1998; Skolnick & Fyfe, 1993; Skolnick & Bayley, 1986). Officers who violate the **code of silence** by reporting fellow officers are shunned, and any transgressions committed by the reporting officer are exposed (Cancino & Enriquez, 2004; Skolnick & Fyfe, 1993). According to Klockars et al. (2006), agencies weaken the **code of silence** if they strongly adhere to specific policies that encourage reporting misconduct and policies that impact both officers and supervisors. The **code of silence** is just one of several factors influencing the ethical conduct of police officers. Other factors include role conflict, hiring practices, the demands of the profession, socialization, personal morality, character, and supervision.

Agencies are turning to **peer intervention** as a way to circumvent the **code of silence**. Training officers how to break down barriers that keep them from intervening during difficult situations on-the-job gives officers a way of stopping misconduct before it happens and alleviating the need for reporting a transgression later. Several programs with promising early results are emerging like the Ethical Policing is Courageous (EPIC) training initiative created by the New Orleans Police Department (NOPD Consent Decree, 2012). One pilot study found that officers who were exposed to the EPIC training were more willing to report a fellow officer and more willing to intervene and prevent misconduct with respect to excessive force (Raines & Merenda, 2022).

Case 7.1: Peer intervention
Imagine you see a student who is clearly cheating on a test. What would you be willing to do: 1. Report the student 2. Pull them aside and tell them how their cheating impacts you 3. Do nothing Does it make a difference whether you know the student, they're a friend, they're someone you dislike? What factors will you take into consideration when making this decision and what might make you more comfortable taking some sort of action?

The Role of the Police Officer

The **role of the police officer** has changed dramatically over time. Initially, the police in the United States were merely average citizens without formal training who stood as night watchmen, collected taxes, caught and punished criminals, and enforced the law. As territories were settled and the railroads expanded westward, private police forces and elected governments kept the peace in the 19th century, but some private citizens in smaller communities became involved in vigilante justice. During the 19th century, however, with the growth of cities and the influx of immigrants, modern policing modeled after the London Metropolitan police force was born. However, the American version was highly politicized and corrupt, relying heavily on favoritism. This was known as the Political Era (Vila & Morris, 1999).

The merit-based system reformed the organizational structure of the police in the early 1900's beginning what is known as the Professional Era of policing that lasted until the 1970's. During the Depression, the role of the police was to protect the public from crime, enforce the law, maintain order, and keep the peace. However, diversity was non-existent, and corruption was still widespread. Many laws were passed improving how officers were chosen and how police organizations were managed, but crime rates continued to increase due to growth in population and urbanization.

With the advent of new technologies in the 1970's, the Professional Era ended, leading to the beginning of Community Policing. Ultimately, the role of the police changed in the 1990's to reflect a growing need for officers to do more than simply respond to criminal activity, but to also work with communities in solving other crime related problems. And so, the concept of community policing was born. Community policing not only demands more interaction between the police and members of the community, it gives members of the community more control over how crime is controlled within their neighborhoods (Vila & Morris, 1999).

Community policing has some drawbacks in that it produces "conflicting demands on police officers and police organizations" (Vila & Morris, 1999, p. xxix). Officers are required to perform multiple roles within a community including counseling, mediating, and enforcing the law. This requires a great deal of autonomy, which can lead to the rise of corruption and/or misconduct (Vila & Morris, 1999). Discretion for the street-level bureaucrat was explored extensively in Chapter 4 of this text.

Case 7.2: Police role conflict
Consider all the things that state troopers do within the scope of their employment. What is the best way to measure their performance? Should a state trooper's job performance be based at all on the number of citations they issue to citizens during any given month? Does counting the number of citations an officer gives out monthly promote public safety, or does it primarily promote increased revenues for the state? What policies should there be in place to adequately measure officer performance with respect to their work that promotes public safety?

Factors that Influence Ethical Awareness and Action

An individual's **ethical awareness** is derived from the individual's values and moral character. Ethical awareness is the basis for an individual's attitudes towards rules, regulations, and policy or **ethical standards**. Klockars et al. (2004) has shown that **ethical awareness** is related to ethical standards and action. An individual's **ethical awareness** ultimately determines whether an individual will take ethical action. The police officer's **ethical awareness** reflects the officer's cognizance of ethical and unethical behavior, as well as the rules, regulations, and policy of the agency. The rules, regulations, and policy provide the backdrop, but the standards by which the officer serves are those that he or she will apply to instances of misconduct. Combined, awareness and standards impact whether the individual is willing to take action (Truelson, 1991; Guy, 1991; Huddleston & Sands, 1995).

Socialization begins for officers during their new recruit training and continues on the job throughout their careers. Measuring the impact of socialization is difficult given the nature of police work. One measure is officer attitude. There are a significant number of qualitative and quantitative studies that explore police officer attitudes (Engel & Worden, 2003). Most of these studies analyze what impact officer attitudes have on police service, arrest rates, detecting crime, use of coercion, and whether officers shirk their duties (Riksheim & Chermak, 1993). Social-psychology research, in general, finds the link between attitudes and behavior is mediated by situational factors such as social norms, peer norms, and peer behavior (Engel & Worden, 2003).

Some examples of influences on officer behavior include seriousness of the offense, gender, and size of agency. There is a positive relationship between the seriousness of the offense and an officer's willingness to arrest. The more serious the offense, the more willing the officer is to make an arrest. Meanwhile, there is a negative relationship between the gender of the suspect and an officer's willingness to make an arrest. Where one suspect is male and the other is female in a domestic violence situation, officers are less likely to make an arrest. With respect to size of agency," some studies have shown that officers from smaller agencies conduct more traffic stops (Riksheim & Chermak, 1993).

In other research, peer behavior and supervisory influence have been shown to impact officer behavior (Engel & Worden, 2003). Officers with high levels of trust, cooperation, group cohesion, and social support will be more successful with community policing (Robinson, 2003). However, officer assignment to community policing does not affect arrest rates (Novak et al., 2002). Also, studies exploring whether statutory language affects arrest rates have found mixed results (Finn et al., 2004). It is unclear whether departmental policies, such as having a pro-arrest policy in domestic disturbances, influence officer behavior (Robinson & Chandek, 2000).

One study found a relationship between negative police officer attitudes and police use of force. Officers who viewed the public, legal restrictions, and supervisors negatively while holding favorable opinions regarding aggressive police tactics and crime fighting were more apt to use coercion in carrying out their duties (Terrill et al., 2003). The officer's attitude towards the victim has a profound effect on an officer's decision to arrest (Robinson & Chandek, 2000). However, no relationship was found between police officers with authoritarian personality traits and police misconduct (Henkel & Sheehan, 1997).

As for socialization effects, there has been some research that suggests the possibility of socialization impacting police misconduct. Limited research has shown a relationship between years of service and cynicism. Officers enter the force with low levels of cynicism which steadily increase during the first ten years on the force. Eventually cynicism declines somewhat creating a relatively curvilinear relationship (Hickman et al., 2004). There is an intriguing similarity with the emergence of unethical behavior. Research shows that the average officer who commits an ethics violation is thirty-two years old with approximately five to ten years of law enforcement experience at the time of his/her transgression (Trautman, 1997).

Implicit bias is another factor that influences arrest decisions. According to the National Institute of Health, **implicit bias** is a person's unintentional prejudice that occurs automatically as a result of attitudes and affects decisions, as well as behaviors. According to Baumgartner et al. (2018), blacks are 63% more likely to be stopped by officers despite driving less than whites. Blacks were also 115% more likely to be searched during a traffic stop than whites. Blacks are also 72% more likely to be arrested than whites despite whites having contraband on them more often than blacks.

Case 7.3: Officer attitudes
Driving while black has been shown repeatedly to exist across the United States, not just in parts of the south or urban areas. What can be done to reduce the emphasis on race when pulling over citizens for traffic stops? How do we combat implicit bias? What are other ways in which implicit bias impacts the justice system?

Situational Factors

Situational factors that affect officer behavior in making arrests include the seriousness of the offense, harm to the victim, and whether or not a weapon is involved in the crime (Robinson & Chandek, 2000). The decision to arrest is made expeditiously in response to a variety of situational factors including seriousness of the offense, characteristics of the suspect and the victim, harm to the victim, and the presence of a weapon. The attitudes about misconduct and an officer's decision to report misconduct reflect a different kind of decision process. It is not unreflective behavior directed at disconnected clients. The decision to report officer misconduct is made after the fact and is directed at peers. Despite these differences, the seriousness of the offense is a factor to consider in evaluating an officer's willingness to report misconduct.

Terrill and Mastrofski (2002) conducted a study that took situational determinants into consideration when observing police officers during arrests. Officers responded to such factors as whether the suspect resisted and safety concerns. Other studies have shown that the more serious the offense involved, the more likely the officer will use force (Garner et al., 1996; Worden, 1995; Kavanagh, 1994; Friedrich, 1977). These studies considered factors such as the seriousness of the offense and violent behavior of the suspect, as well as other factors such as race, intoxication of the suspect, presence of bystanders, and whether the officer initiated the contact.

Case 7.4: Officer use of force
Two police officers on foot patrol surprise a suspect who is attempting to break into an automobile The suspect flees. They chase the suspect for about two blocks before apprehending them by tackling them and wrestling them to the ground. After they are under control both officers punch them a couple of times in the stomach as punishment for fleeing and resisting (Klockers et al., 2000). How serious is the behavior of the two officers? Would you be willing to report this behavior as a bystander? or as a fellow officer?

Organizational Factors

As discussed in Chapter 4, organizational factors (size of agency, departmental bureaucratization, and police presence) can impact officer behavior. Alpert and MacDonald (2001) studied the impact that agency-level characteristics have on police use of force. Agency-level characteristics included whether an agency was accredited by the Commission on Accreditation for Law Enforcement Agencies, whether an agency was accredited by its state, whether the agency was unionized, whether an agency used data collected on use of force for management and administrative purposes, and whether supervisors or individual officers completed use of force forms. The study controlled for level of danger within the jurisdiction and the region within the U.S.

Alpert and MacDonald (2001) found that some agency characteristics impact an officer's use of force. Agencies that required supervisors to fill out use of force forms experienced lower rates of force by officers. Accreditation and unionization did not impact an officer's use of force, however, and those agencies that used data for management and administrative purposes experienced higher rates of force by officers. The agency characteristics utilized in the Alpert and MacDonald (2001) study offer some partial support for the effect that **organizational factors** have on police behavior.

But what of corruption within an organization that is more widespread and not simply one officer acting alone? Frank Serpico was a NYPD officer in the 1960s and 1970s. He bounced between several different precincts during his career coming across widespread corruption within the police ranks everywhere he went. Serpico tried to avoid joining in the schemes, but this just made his colleagues suspicious of him. Eventually Serpico told his story to the *New York Times* which led to the creation of a panel known as the Knapp Commission charged with investigating police corruption. Serpico testified before the Knapp Commission which in turn led to the development of Internal Affairs for investigating police misconduct.

Case 7.5
A police officer, who happens to be a very good auto mechanic, is scheduled to work during coming holidays. A supervisor offers to give them these days off, if they agree to tune-up the supervisor's personal car. Evaluate the SUPERVISOR'S behavior and the impact this behavior will have on the attitudes of the officers within the agency (Klockers et al., 2000).

Individual Factors

Individual factors such as length of service, rank and job assignment affect officer behavior (McElvain and Kposowa 2004). Van Wart (1998) recognizes the impact that expertise has on the amount of discretion afforded to public administrators. Administrators with higher levels of expertise enjoy more discretion and decision-making within an agency. For example, officers and detectives are different. While becoming a detective is considered a promotion, this position generally does not have supervisory responsibilities. Still, in a few studies that have looked at differences in specialization of job assignment in police agencies, no appreciable difference between how police officers carry out their duties in specialized versus non-specialized departments was found (Mastrofski et al., 1995; Novak et al., 2002).

What impact does expertise have on police officers? Controlling for race, gender, and age, officers with five to nine years of experience were twelve times more likely to be investigated for misuse of force than their colleagues who had served for twenty years or more (McElvain and Kposowa, 2004). Race and gender were not found to be a significant factor in predicting misuse of force investigations, however, age and prior investigation were both significant. The younger the officer, the more likely to be investigated for misuse of force, and officers who had been investigated at least once were more likely to be investigated again during their careers (McElvain and Kposowa, 2004). Unfortunately, there is a lack of research regarding the impact that rank, supervisory position and job assignment have on police behavior. Only a few studies have looked at differences in specialization of job assignment in police agencies and found no appreciable difference between how police officers carry out their duties in specialized versus non-specialized departments (Mastrofski et al., 1995; Novak et al., 2002).

An officer's supervisory position appears to impact how serious that officer views misconduct. Supervisors view misconduct as more serious than non-supervisors, which is not surprising considering supervisors have been on the job longer and may be the individuals responsible for administering punishment for officer misconduct. Being on the job longer does not necessarily mean officers view misconduct more seriously as their careers progress. There is a curvilinear relationship between an officer's attitudes towards misconduct and years of service controlling for supervisory position. A socialization process and/or negative experiences during the first six years of service seem to undercut the ideals of new recruits. Further support for this is found with non-supervisory officers with one to six years of service who are less likely to report misconduct than officers who have been in service longer (Raines, 2010).

Case 7.6
For cases 7.4, 7.5, and 7.7 in this chapter, what punishment do you think should follow from the behavior engaged in by the officers in those scenarios? What punishment do you think would follow?

Police Culture

Paoline (2001) identifies five types of police officers based on attitudes and background characteristics. These five types are Tough-Cops, Clean-Beat Crime-Fighters, Avoiders, Problem-Solvers, and Professionals. These groups affect relationships with citizens and supervisors, attitudes towards legal restrictions and community policing, and attitudes towards their role in society (Paoline, 2001).

Tough-Cops hold negative attitudes towards citizens, supervisors, legal restrictions, order maintenance, and community policing. Tough cops may be more prone to **noble cause corruption**, being more willing to ignore legal restrictions that they disdain in order to achieve what they perceive to be a just outcome. This type of officer believes in pursuing the law enforcement role, aggressive policing and only handling serious violations. **Clean-Beat Crime-Fighters** are similar to **Tough-Cops**, but value legal restrictions, order maintenance, and pursuing all types of illegal behavior (Paoline, 2001).

Avoiders are also like **Tough-Cops**, but they are neutral in their attitudes towards supervisors. **Avoiders**, as the name implies, avoid work and aggressive behavior to keep from drawing attention to themselves. **Problem Solvers** and **Professionals** have positive relationships with citizens and supervisors. Both types of police officers value order maintenance and community policing. **Problem-Solvers**, however, see legal restrictions as an impediment to their work and are neutral in their attitude toward their role in enforcing the law. **Problem-Solvers** also believe in focusing their energies on serious problems (Paoline, 2001).

Paoline's research questions the single moral order concept of police culture. He highlights the differences in attitudes within police culture and identifies an additional seven subcultures in his research. Van Maanen (1973) analyzes **stages of cultural socialization** for police officers instead of categorizing officers as Paoline and Wilson have done. According to Van Maanen (1973), there are four stages of police socialization into the organization, which include a pre-entry choice, introduction, encounter, and metamorphosis stages.

The first stage, **pre-entry choice**, acknowledges the individual's choice to become a police officer. This stage recognizes that most individuals who choose to become police officers hold similar values as those values held within the law enforcement profession. The second stage, **introduction**, involves the new recruit's training phase within formal instruction. The third stage, **encounter**, includes the new recruits on-the-job training with a senior police officer once initial new recruit training is completed. In the final stage, **metamorphosis**, the officer adapts to the nature of police work and is impacted by peer reinforcement of group norms.

While these four stages were first created over thirty years ago, the stages are still accurate today (Adcox, 2000). The stages focus on the beginning of an officer's career where the primary socialization occurs. An officer's ethical decision making is most impacted within stage three. Relying in part on Sykes (1994), Adcox highlights the importance of stage three:

> These initial experiences can either set the stage for ethical behavior or teach the rationalization of inappropriate conduct. The actions of others speak far louder than any written policy, and the peer group becomes the most powerful conveyor of the unwritten code of conduct. (Adcox, 2000, p. 22)

Stage three, or the period when officers are receiving on-the-job training, is critical to the development of an officer's ethical decision making. Stage three is when peers inculcate norms as an "unwritten code of conduct" (Adcox, 2000, p. 22). Individual and organizational factors impact individual attitudes and values shaped by the organization's structure and culture. These factors impact officers through hiring, socialization, and training.

There is conflicting research regarding the impact the socialization process has on an officer's ethical orientation. Research indicates that new recruits have a significantly different ethical perspective from that of seasoned officers. According to Catlin and Maupin (2004), new recruits tend to be idealistic in their ethical orientation while officers who have been on the job for at least one year are more relativistic in their ethical orientation. This difference highlights the importance of how officers are hired, formally trained, and ultimately integrated into the police culture.

An officer's personality, the hiring process, and their formal training each play a role in shaping the ethical decision-making of this street-level bureaucrat (Lyman, 1999; Kraska & Kappeler, 1998). The officer's personality can be measured through the Myers-Briggs Type Indicator (MBTI). Stages of moral development are commonly measured through the Defining Issues Test (DIT). These two tests are not commonly utilized in the hiring process for police officers (Hughes, 2003). Whether these tests should be used in hiring decisions remains to be seen, however, these tests do offer insight into the police officer psyche.

Case 7.7
At 2 A.M. a police officer, who is on duty, is driving his patrol car on a deserted road. He sees a vehicle that has been driven off the road and is stuck in a ditch. He approaches the vehicle and observes that the driver is not hurt but is obviously intoxicated. He also finds that the driver is a police officer. Instead of reporting this accident and offense he transports the driver to his home (Klockers et al., 2000). This type of misconduct is called **nonfeasance** – failure to act when there is a duty to act. What would you do if you were the officer in this situation?

Police Tactics

Deception in interrogations is surprisingly legal in the United States. Officers can give suspects misinformation to get information needed to solve crimes. According to Sissela Bok (1999), lying is justified in extreme circumstances like protecting human life and within criminal contexts, but not without limitation. A majority of interrogations last less than an hour without the need for special tactics like deception (Feld, 2006; Leo, 1995). One study found that presenting a suspect with false evidence of their guilt can be helpful in obtaining a confession, but not as successful as relying on other tactics like praising the suspect or offering justifications and excuses for their behavior (Leo, 1995). The use of deception raises questions such as when is it appropriate and/or necessary in solving a crime or garnering a confession, when does the use of deception become oppressive, and when does it become manipulation that leads to a false confession?

The **Reid Technique** is an approach to interrogation that is commonly used by law enforcement. It is controversial because it can lead to false confessions. The **Reid Technique** focuses on a suspect's behavioral cues during interrogation that will tell the investigator whether the suspect is lying and teaches interrogators to presume guilt during interrogations. Presuming guilt is problematic, as is relying on visual behavioral cues as they are hard to interpret. A suspect who is nervous may look like they're hiding something when they're simply nervous being interrogated by the police. Age, maturity, language skills, and intelligence influence susceptibility to coercion particularly where oppressive interrogation tactics are employed by interrogators (Moore and Fitzimmons, 2011). As the **Reid Technique** was first developed in the 1950s, has it become obsolete? Some countries (Canada and Britain) have shifted to different interrogation methods that do not begin by assuming the suspect is guilty and avoid the use of deception during interrogation.

Entrapment occurs when undercover police investigations go too far and induce potential suspects to commit crimes they might not have committed otherwise but for the officers enticement. There are two basic tenets of **entrapment** – one that focuses on protecting innocent individuals from being tricked into committing a crime they wouldn't have otherwise committed and another that focuses on deterring law enforcement from entrapping innocent citizens. Sting operations, decoy operations, buy/sell and bust, and other types of deceit are commonly used by law enforcement to catch criminals in unlawful acts, however, determining when a line has been crossed and entrapment has occurred is virtually impossible (Colquitt, 2004).

Case 7.8: To Catch a Predator
This Dateline NBC series ran from 2004 to 2007 and focused on creating sting operations to lure men into meeting with and potentially having sex with minors who were portrayed by adults online in fake accounts. The show was successful attracting over 150 men into sting operations across 10 investigation sting sites in the U.S. The series was canceled shortly after one of the suspected predators, Bill Conradt, committed suicide while being served with a warrant in his home. He was a district attorney in Texas who exchanged online conversations and photos with an adult posing as a 13-year-old boy but had never shown up to the sting site in person. Discuss the ethical issues raised in this case including: 1. The role of the media in reporting news versus creating it as is the case with this series. 2. When does the media go too far in investigating crimes or is this the job of an investigative journalist? 3. Is this series more about investigating or ratings? 4. Is broadcasting these sting operations and exposing the suspected predators a form of punishment? 5. Is luring men to a site using fake online accounts is entrapment? When does a sting operation cross the line?

Conclusion

Police are a unique group of individuals because they seek to prevent crime as their career. Officers are entrusted with a noble responsibility in our society - to protect other members of society much like fire fighters. Officers are required to safeguard property, avoid use of excessive force, avoid corruption, use consistent and wise discretion, keep confidences, cooperate with other law enforcement agencies, and exhibit exemplary behavior off duty. The majority of officers accomplish their goals effectively, serving their communities honorably. However, even a small number of incidents is a matter of concern given the nature of law enforcement's role in society.

Debate Topics for In-Class Discussion

1. Defunding the police
   a. *Pro* – moving funds from policing to social services can cut down on aggressive policing tactics and increase community health and wellness
   b. *Con* – moving funds away from policing will limit police training designed to greatly reduce misuse of force
2. Whether an officer's prior use of cannabis should bar employment in law enforcement
   a. *Pro* – officers must be held to a higher standard so they won't be tempted while on the job
   b. *Con* – it's challenging to find individuals who want to go into police work which would then severely limit hiring pools

Terms

Reasons why officers might commit unethical acts
Peer intervention
Role of the police officer
Ethical awareness
Ethical standards
Implicit bias
Situational factors
Organizational factors
Individual factors
Tough-cops
Noble cause corruption
Clean-Beat Crime Fighters
Avoiders
Problem Solvers
Professionals
Stages of cultural socialization
Pre-entry choice stage
Introduction stage
Encounter stage
Metamorphosis stage
Deception in interrogations
Reid Technique
Entrapment
Code of silence
Nonfeasance

References

Adcox, K.L. (2000, January). Doing Bad Things for Good Reasons. *The Police Chief*, 17-28.

Alpert, G.P., & MacDonald, J.M. (2001). Police Use of Force: An Analysis of Organizational Characteristics. Justice Quarterly, 18(2), 393-409.

Baumgartner, F. R., Epp, D. A., & Shoub, K. (2018). *Suspect citizens: What 20 million traffic stops tell us about policing and race.* Cambridge University Press.

Bok, S. (1999). *Lying: Moral choice in public and private life*. Vintage.

Cancino, J.M., & Enriquez, R. (2004). A Qualitative Analysis of Officer Peer Retaliation. *Policing: An International Journal of Police Strategies and Management, 27*(3), 320-340.

Catlin, D.W., & Maupin, J.R. (2004). A Two Cohort Study of the Ethical Orientations of State Police Officers. *Policing: An International Journal of Police Strategies and Management, 27*(3), 289-301.

Colquitt, J. A. (2004). Rethinking entrapment. *American Criminal Law Review, 41(4),* 1389-1438.

Consent Decree Regarding the New Orleans Police Department. (2012). Retrieved from http://www.laed.uscourts.gov/Consent/NewOrleans Decree.pdf

Engel, R.S., & Worden, R.E. (2003). Police Officers' Attitudes, Behavior, and Supervisory Influences: An Analysis of Problem Solving. *Criminology, 41*(1), 131-166.

Farrell, D. (1983). Exit, Voice, Loyalty, and Neglect as Responses to Job Dissatisfaction - A Multidimensional-Scaling Study. Academy of Management Journal, 26(4), 596-607.

Feld, B. C. (2006). Police interrogation of juveniles: An empirical study of policy and practice. *J. Crim. L. & Criminology, 97*, 219.

Finn, M.A., Blackwell, B.S., Stalans, L.J., Studdard, S., & Dugan, L. (2004). Dual Arrest Decisions in Domestic Violence Cases: The Influence of Departmental Policies. Crime & Delinquency, 50(4), 565-589.

Friedrich, R.J. (1977). The Impact of Organizational, Individual, and Situational Factors on Police Behavior. University of Michigan.

Garner, J.H., Buchanan, J., Schade, T., & Hepburn, J. (1996). Understanding the Continuum of Force by and Against the Police. *National Institute of Justice.*

Guy, M.E. (1991). Using High Reliability Management to Promote Ethical Decision Making. In Anonymous, (pp. 185-204). San Francisco: Jossey-Bass.

Henkel, J., & Sheehan, E.P. (1997). Relation of Police Misconduct to Authoritarianism. *Journal of Social Behavior & Personality, 12*(2), 551-556.

Hickman, M.J., Piquero, N.L., & Piquero, A.R. (2004). The Validity of Niederhoffer's Cynicism Scale. *Journal of Criminal Justice, 32*, 1-13.

Hirschman, A.O. (1970). Exit, Voice and Loyalty: Responses to Decline in Firms, Organizations and States. (ed.). Boston: Harvard University Press.

Huddleston, M.W., & Sands, J.C. (1995). Enforcing Administrative Ethics. The Annals of the American Academy of Political and Social Science, 537, 139-149.

Hughes, T.T. (2003). Jordan v. The City of New London, Police Hiring and IQ. Policing: An International Journal of Police Strategies and Management, 26(2), 298-312.

Human Rights Watch Staff. (1998). *Human Rights Watch World Report 1999.* Human Rights Watch.

Kavanagh, J. (1994). The Occurrence of Force in Arrest Encounters. Rutgers University.

Kelly, J. & Nichols, M. (2020, June 11). Tarnished Brass. *U.S. Today.*

Klockars, C.B., Ivkovic, S.K., & Haberfeld, M. (2006). *Enhancing Police Integrity*. (ed.). New York: Springer Publishing.

Klockars, C.B., Ivkovic, S.K., & Haberfeld, M. (2004). *The Contours of Police Integrity*. (ed.). Thousand Oaks: SAGE Publications.

Kraska, P.B., & Kappeler, V.E. (1998). A Textual Critique of Community Policing: Police Adaptation to High Modernity. *Policing: An International Journal of Police Strategies and Management, 21*(2), 293-313.

Leo, R. A. (1995). Inside the interrogation room. *J. Crim. L. & Criminology, 86*, 266.

Lyman, M. (1999). *The Police: An Introduction*. (Ed.). New York: Prentice Hall.

Mastrofski, S.D., Worden, R.E., & Snipes, J.B. (1995). Law Enforcement in a Time of Community Policing. *Criminology, 33*(4), 539-603.

McElvain, J.P., & Kposowa, A.J. (2004). Police Officer Characteristics and Internal Affairs Investigations for Use of Force Allegations. *Journal of Criminal Justice, 32*, 265-279.

Moore, T. E., & Fitzsimmons, C. L. (2011). Justice imperiled: False confessions and the Reid technique. *Crim. LQ, 57*, 509.

National Institute of Health. Department of Health and Human Services. *Implicit Bias*. https://diversity.nih.gov/sociocultural-factors/implicit-bias

Novak, K.J., Frank, J., Smith, B.W., & Engel, R.S. (2002). Revisiting the Decision to Arrest: Comparing Beat and Community Officers. *Crime & Delinquency, 48*(1), 70-98.

Paoline III, E.A. (2001). *Rethinking Police Culture: Officers' Occupational Attitudes*. (ed.). New York: LFB Scholarly Publishing LLC.

Raines, J. (2010). *Ethics in policing: Misconduct and integrity*. Jones & Bartlett Learning.

Raines, J. B., & Merenda, F. (2022). Evaluating implementation of the EPIC peer bystander intervention program in basic law enforcement training (BLET). *Police Practice and Research, 24*(3), 384-396.

Riksheim, E.C., & Chermak, S.M. (1993). Causes of Police Behavior Revisited. *Journal of Criminal Justice, 21*, 353-382.

Robinson, A.L. (2003). The Impact of Police Social Capital on Officer Performance of Community Policing. *Policing: An International Journal of Police Strategies and Management, 26*(4), 656-689.

Robinson, A.L., & Chandek, M.S. (2000). The Domestic Violence Arrest Decision: Examining Demographic, Attitudinal, and Situational Variables. *Crime & Delinquency, 46*(1), 18-37.

Rusbult, C.E., Zembrodt, I.M., & Gunn, L.K. (1982). Exit, Voice, Loyalty, and Neglect - Responses To Dissatisfaction in Romantic Involvements. *Journal of Personality and Social Psychology, 43*(6), 1230-1242.

Skolnick, J., & Bayley, D. (1986). *The New Blue Line: Police Innovation in Six American Cities.* (ed.). New York: Free Press.

Skolnick, J., & Fyfe, J. (1993). *Above the Law: Police and the Excessive Use of Force.* (ed.). New York: Maxwell MacMillan International.

Steinberg, S.S., & Austern, D.T. (1990). *Government, Ethics, and Managers: A Guide to Solving Ethical Dilemmas in the Public Sector.* (ed.). Westport: Praeger.

Sykes, G.W. (1994, Summer). That's the Way We Do Things Around Here. *Law Enforcement Ethics Center Newsletter.*

Tapp, S., & Davis, E. (2022). Contacts between police and the public, 2020. *Bureau of Justice Statics Report, NCJ, 304527.*

Terrill, W., & Mastrofski, S. D. (2002). Situational and officer-based determinants of police coercion. *Justice quarterly, 19*(2), 215-248.

Terrill, W., Paoline III, E.A., & Manning, P.K. (2003). Police Culture and Coercion. *Criminology, 41*(4), 1003-1034.

Trautman, N.E. *The National Law Enforcement Officer Disciplinary Research Project.* (1997). Anonymous. The Ethics Institute.

Truelson, J. A. (1991). New strategies for institutional controls. *Ethical frontiers in public management,* 225-242.

Van Maanen, J. (1973). Observations of the Making of a Policeman. *Human Organization, 32,* 407-418.

Van Wart, M. (1998). *Changing Public Sector Values.* (Ed.). New York: Garland Publishing, Inc.

Vila, B., & Morris, C. (1999). *The Role of Police in American Society: A Documentary History.* (ed.). Westport: Greenwood Press.

Withey, M.J., & Cooper, W.H. (1989). Predicting Exit, Voice, Loyalty, and Neglect. Administrative Science Quarterly, 34(4), 521-539.

Worden, R.E. (1995). *The Causes of Police Brutality: Theory and Evidence on Police Use of Force*. In W. Geller & H. Toch (Ed.). Washington, DC: Police Executive Research Forum.

Chapter 8
Ethical Issues in the Courts

Chapter Objectives

1. Expose students to the rules of professional conduct for attorneys and judges.
2. Analyze various moral dilemmas that occur procedurally within the criminal court system.
3. Discuss the various ways to hold attorneys and judges accountable for misconduct.
4. Consider the impact that misconduct by prosecutors, defense counsel, and judges has on defendants and society.
5. Compare moral dilemmas of prosecutors, defense attorneys, and judges.

Introduction

In 1983, Kenneth Waters was convicted of murdering Katherina Brow in Ayer, Massachusetts. His sister, Betty Anne, went to college, law school, and passed the bar exam so that she could represent her brother. With help from the Innocence Project, Betty Anne later finds evidence that exonerates her brother. The Waters case, while exceptional, is an example of some of the problems in the court system that can lead to wrongful conviction. The case led to a popular movie depicting the events that highlights some of these moral dilemmas. The court system has a plethora of other ethical dilemmas faced every day by victims, defendants, lawyers, judges, and administrative staff. This chapter addresses some of those dilemmas.

Courts face moral dilemmas with respect to how defendants are processed through the system, as well as how victims are treated. Additionally, prosecutors, defense counsel, and judges each face moral dilemmas unique to their respective roles within the justice system. As was the case with law enforcement, discretion for each of these actors in the courtroom can lead to misconduct. All three actors within the justice system are attorneys at their core and bound by formal rules called the Model Rules of Professional Conduct (Model Rules). Lawyers are required to pass a separate, standardized exam demonstrating proficiency of knowledge on the Model Rules in addition to passing the traditional state bar exam prior to licensure. The sections that follow focus on moral dilemmas that arise within court systems, as well as ethical issues faced by prosecutors, defense counsel, and judges.

Model Rules

Originally called Canons of Professional Ethics, later called Model Code of Professional Responsibility, now referred to as Model Rules of Professional Conduct, and typically referred to as the **Model Rules**, attorneys and judges are held to the standards of behavior established by the American Bar Association (ABA) which also provides assistance to states with respect to attorney licensure (ABA, 2006). Broadly speaking, attorneys working in the criminal justice setting have an obligation to provide counsel to defendants regardless of whether defendants can pay for legal services which goes beyond merely relying on public defender offices. Many large law practices provide attorneys solely devoted to representing clients in both criminal and civil matters pro bono, or free of charge as a way to give back to society in the spirit of the **Model Rules** (Love, 2001).

One of the biggest complaints by defendants is **lack of communication** with their attorney. Given the nature of legal practice – constantly in meetings and/or court – it can be difficult to get your attorney's attention. The **Model Rules** requires keeping defendants "**reasonably informed**" regarding any offers of plea bargaining, also referred to as **informed consent**. There are no definitive ways to determine what reasonably informed is, however, it is clear that attorneys do need to give notice to the defendant, give the defendant time to consider the offer and not merely a few minutes, and the defendant's consent to any plea bargain must be informed, preferably in writing by the attorney to the client.

Attorneys must also be explicit in garnering an **informed consent** from the defendant. And attorneys must adhere to **confidentiality** on behalf of the defendant, not disclosing conversations held with their clients, unless disclosure will prevent future crimes and/or harm. If aiding the defendant leads the defense counsel into unknowingly committing fraud, then the attorney must remove themselves from the case. Also, the attorney cannot represent a defendant where a **conflict of interest** arises, which typically means the attorney has represented someone who has some type of relationship with the defendant. The defendant, however, can waive the conflict of interest after full disclosure by defense counsel (Love, 2001).

Accountability for defense counsel not associated with public defender offices is the same as for civil attorneys. The **Model Rules** govern how clients can be charged fees requiring transparency and communication so that clients are not surprised by one huge bill at the end of services. Regardless of whether a defendant relies on a public defender or private defense counsel, the defendant has the power to fire their attorney and the power of self-representation. The judge will typically try to dissuade defendants from doing either as it can greatly slow down the process and lead to more errors in the case. Attorneys can also withdraw from representation in rare circumstances and judges are reluctant to allow withdrawal without compelling reasons. Accountability for prosecutors, public defenders, and judges are discussed in the sections that follow.

Case 8.1: Attorney Withdrawal
An attorney is representing a client in an upcoming hearing to resolve several issues in a case that might end up finally resolving a case that has been languishing for over a year in the system. The attorney is about to move to another state and has tried to secure alternate representation for the defendant with no luck. The hearing is about a week prior to the attorney moving out of the jurisdiction and the attorney has shut down her law practice and discontinued her malpractice insurance. Should the attorney represent the defendant in the hearing? Should the judge excuse the attorney under the circumstances? Does it matter whether the case is criminal as the example here suggests or civil like in a divorce case, for example?

Legal Rules and Procedures

The **rules of evidence** require lawyers to avoid the presentation of false evidence where the lawyer knows it to be false. Seems straightforward, but when does an attorney know evidence that is being presented is false evidence? For example, a defendant who professes innocence may demand to take the stand and could potentially be lying. The defense counsel cannot aid in perjured testimony, but also cannot prevent a defendant from testifying if that is their wish. So, the defense attorney must have some evidence that the defendant is perjuring themselves during direct examination by defense counsel or otherwise allow the defendant to testify.

It is also well known that when a witness is asked to identify the perpetrator of a crime, they will always point to whoever is sitting at the defense table even when the defendant may not be sitting there at all (Tanford, 2001). Eyewitness testimony is not terribly reliable, in general, but a prosecutor will consistently rely on eyewitness testimony regardless because it is highly impactful on jury decision-making. Since eyewitness testimony can be challenged through cross-examination and the use of experts, it is still considered acceptable for prosecutors to introduce it as evidence in criminal trials (Kassin et al., 2001).

Pretrial release is another area of contention within the criminal justice system. In 2020, prior to the pandemic, New York was just beginning to implement new bail reform legislation that promoted releasing non-violent defendants without securing bail. The new law was designed to decrease jail populations within a system that discriminates against the poor and people of color. Since then, tensions have arisen over defendants who were released only to commit more crimes, as well as in some rare instances violent crimes.

As we've discussed in earlier chapters, moral dilemmas spring from competing values. With bail reform the protection of society hangs in the balance. On the one hand, incarcerating overwhelming numbers of arrestees for extended periods of time comes with many social costs including increased recidivism. On the other hand, releasing arrestees without some type of intervention in place of jail time still leads to recidivism. And even with bail reform measures in place, many judges were reluctant to immediately release defendants and openly defied the law or found ways to circumvent it.

Case 8.2: Eyewitness testimony
You are a prosecutor for a case where a 17-year-old is facing adult murder charges in a shooting where the primary evidence is eyewitness testimony. You can charge the defendant with a lesser charge than premeditated murder and encourage a settlement, but the community is outraged about the murder as the victim was well known and liked by many. What factors would you take into consideration in making your decision? Prior convictions of the defendant? The reliability of the eyewitnesses – what would make you comfortable relying solely on eyewitness testimony? Consider various circumstances where you would feel comfortable and circumstances where you would not feel comfortable moving forward with a trial.

Diversion Courts

Specialty **diversion courts**, commonly referred to as **treatment courts**, were born from a reimagining of existing rules and procedures in many cases and evolved over time through the creation of new rules and procedures. Judge Steven Leifman from Miami-Dade County first recognized the repeating cycle of drug addiction and mental health issues that plagued the defendants in his courtroom. He created the first **drug treatment court** and the first **mental health treatment court**. The idea is that instead of putting defendants in jail or prison they complete drug and/or mental health treatment in programs that last anywhere from a year to 18 months on average. Once completed, participants in these programs graduate from them and have their original charges expunged.

Defendants, referred to as clients or participants once transferred into the program, progress through a series of three to five phases with the typical court having four phases. During the initial phases the participant comes to court every week before the judge overseeing the treatment court, engages in treatment, is tested for substance use frequently, and is subject to whatever recommendations the treatment team recommends. Sometimes the recommendation is to enter into short term or long-term, in-patient care at an approved rehabilitative facility. Many participants also rely on **Medication-Assisted Treatment (MAT)** which is a way for participants to curb their cravings for illicit substances and eventually titrate off of the **MAT** closer to the end of their treatment court experience.

While these programs have been largely successful in reducing recidivism and giving participants in them their lives back, they do have some drawbacks. First, judges who oversee a **diversion court** docket have strong opinions regarding how their docket should be managed meaning that these courts vary widely depending on the jurisdiction and the judge. **Treatment courts** are seen as a type of therapeutic jurisprudence and judges are not therapists. Some judges struggle with finding the right balance of providing adequate support for participants in their programs who come to court weekly to check in with the judge regarding progress in the program.

Other issues that arise in **treatment courts** include how to manage participant compliance within these programs. The current model being promoted is one of **harm reduction** which backs off on punishment and accountability for participants in the programs. While treatment courts are a marked movement away from punishment, holding participants accountable through the use of mandatory and frequent drug screenings is critical to their recovery. Some rehabilitation facilities are unwilling to supervise participants while giving urine samples because they insist it is traumatizing, but participants are notorious for switching out urine if given the opportunity. And while relapse is inevitable for many participants in these programs, at what point should judges send participants back to their original criminal court judge and release them from the treatment court for non-compliance?

Case 8.3: Treatment courts
A participant in a drug treatment court has failed his drug test this week, but he shows up for court as is required each week. Fentanyl was found in his drug test which concerns the judge that his participant could be at high risk to overdose if he doesn't go to an in-patient facility quickly. Unfortunately, it takes at least a couple of weeks and usually longer to find a facility that has an available bed and get the participant screened and approved for admittance. Should the judge incarcerate the participant until a bed opens to keep him safe? The state has indicated that it doesn't want judges to use jail for this purpose as it can be seen as punishment. It can also scare other participants into not showing up for court for fear of being put in jail if they fail a drug test. What would you do if you were the judge? What factors would you take into consideration in making your decision?

Ethical Issues for Prosecutors

In both an adversarial court system like the United States and an inquisitorial system found in Europe, prosecutors have a lot of discretion. In the United States, **prosecutorial discretion** is critical with respect to three main areas which include whether to prosecute, which criminal charges will be brought, and when to discontinue prosecution (Albonetti, 1987). Prosecutors get to determine whether they will prosecute a case as they have a high burden of proof to meet in criminal cases. Prosecutors determine charges they will bring against a defendant typically taking into consideration the evidence available and whether they feel they can achieve a conviction. In addition to the three main areas of discretion, prosecutors routinely make recommendations to the judge regarding whether to secure bail and what bail should be set at in a case which has become more challenging in a post bail reform world. Prosecutors have an impact on which cases will be referred to treatment courts in many jurisdictions. The prosecutor will also make sentencing recommendations to the judge in plea bargaining cases that will be taken into consideration along with any presentencing report provided by probation, as well as arguments made by defense counsel.

In European countries that rely on inquisitorial systems, the prosecutor has discretion in collecting the evidence from the victim and the accused. They can choose to be helpful and sympathetic or not, which can have a big impact on whether a case progresses through the system. In less serious cases, the prosecutor's influence is primarily prior to the bench trial where the judge takes over and the prosecutor will not be present in these types of cases unlike in the United States. Prosecutors in inquisitorial courts are more likely to be present during the presentation of the case in court where there is a serious offense.

As a result of **prosecutorial discretion**, ethical issues arise when prosecutors decide not to prosecute a case in an adversarial system or where they decide to not be helpful to the victim or the accused in an inquisitorial system. For example, in an adversarial system with rape cases many jurisdictions with limited resources may decide to not send rape kits to labs for analysis. The reasoning behind this decision is that these are tough cases to get a conviction in particularly where the defendant denies any wrongdoing. Victims are routinely accused of being not credible and often wrongfully blamed for being partially responsible simply for being intoxicated at the time of the sexual assault (Spohn et al., 2014). Since the prosecutor has discretion over whether to bring a case to trial versus plea bargaining or simply dropping a matter altogether, victims in these cases typically have little to no voice in the decision-making process and cannot legally challenge a decision to not prosecute in a case (*Linda R. S. v. Richard D.*, 1973).

Discretion in decision making can often lead to issues of racial and gender bias. Race and sex of both the victim and suspect impact whether a prosecutor will allow charges to move forward in a case. In the United States, where a victim is white and/or the perpetrator is black or Hispanic, prosecutors have higher rates of allowing charges to move forward (Baker & Hassan, 2021; Baldus et al., 1990; Smith & Levinson, 2011; Sorensen & Wallace, 1999). Meanwhile, rates of minorities being diverted to treatment courts lags by 7% to over 20% as compared to minorities who have been arrested, on probation or parole, or incarcerated. As the decision to divert a defendant to treatment courts depends on a number of different influences including judges and administrators, prosecutors are only partially responsible for these disparities (Marlowe, 2013).

According to *Berger v. United States* (1935, p. 88), it is the prosecutor's:

> duty to refrain from improper methods calculated to produce a wrongful conviction as it is to use every legitimate means to bring about a just one.

Prosecutorial misconduct occurs when a prosecutor acting on behalf of the government engages in improper methods that violate a defendant's constitutional rights in order to win a case. Crossing the line for a prosecutor can happen when cross examining a witness, withholding exculpatory evidence, manipulating evidence, as well as when using race as a factor in choosing jurors, deciding to charge a defendant, or determining whether to ask for bail (Henning, 1999).

Case 8.4: Prosecutorial Misconduct
While District Attorney for Durham, North Carolina, Mike Nifong brought rape, sexual assault, and kidnapping charges against 3 members of the Duke Lacrosse team. The charges were based on allegations made by a stripper hired by the Lacrosse team. The allegations by the stripper were later found to be false through an investigation by the state Attorney General and Nifong was found to have refused to hear exculpatory evidence provided by the defendants, withheld exculpatory DNA evidence, and manipulated witnesses. Nifong was disbarred, resigned from his position as District Attorney, and was later held in contempt of court for a variety of offenses related to his handling of the case. The 3 members of the Duke Lacrosse team incurred legal expenses of over $3 million and spent a year defending their reputations after having been forced out of Duke University. Was Nifong's punishment appropriate under the circumstances?

Ethical Issues for Defense Counsel

Caseloads for public defenders in the United States can be overwhelming leading to a lack of attention paid to each client. A 2007 caseload analysis of public defender offices in the United States found that on average they represent between 327 to 358 clients per year (Farole & Langton, 2010). One study found that public defenders with higher felony caseloads resulted in increased pretrial detention rates and incarceration sentences (Gottlieb & Arnold, 2021). In Louisiana caseloads were so overburdensome for public defenders that the courts found a rebuttable presumption of **ineffective assistance of counsel** (*State v. Peart*, 1993). Public defenders' offices in Florida, Louisiana, Missouri, New Mexico, and Tennessee have started refusing to take new cases because of overburdensome caseloads (Gross, 2017). This, of course, leaves those defendants stranded without any counsel which begs the question is no counsel better than overburdened, ineffective counsel?

Discretion for public defenders in terms of advising their clients can also be a source of ethical misconduct. Plea bargaining is the primary method of disposing of cases in the justice system. Public defenders must decide between encouraging a plea deal versus encouraging going to trial. Judges are also more inclined to promote plea agreements as trials are time consuming processes within an already overburdened system and defense attorneys don't want to alienate judges that they regularly come into contact with every week. And then there are **treatment courts** which are designed to help take some pressure off the correctional system by diverting defendants from jails and prisons. Public defenders are sometimes conflicted about advising their clients to choose treatment court over a traditional sentence particularly in misdemeanor cases where sentences are low and treatment courts typically take 12-18 months for completion. When making this decision, how does one weigh the value of probation, incarceration, length of time in treatment, and engagement in programs that encourage sobriety against one another?

In the United States, defendants have a Sixth Amendment **right to counsel** and a **duty to represent their clients zealously**. Failure to provide zealous representation to a client is known as ineffective assistance of counsel. Defendants can make a claim of **ineffective assistance of counsel** and if successful can receive a new trial. **Ineffective assistance of counsel** includes not questioning potential witnesses during the discovery phase of trial, not having DNA evidence examined, not investigating evidence and/or challenging the prosecutor's evidence, and not staying awake during hearings and other court proceedings. **Ineffective assistance of counsel** can occur even when caseloads for defense counsel are not overly burdensome. For example, in a smaller jurisdiction where violent felonies may be less common and public defender offices may be nonexistent, local attorneys step up to represent indigent clients in cases they have little to no experience handling. Attorneys can also be ineffective when going through trauma in their own personal lives (divorce, death of a family member, alcoholism/drug abuse) while representing clients.

Meanwhile, in inquisitorial systems, the accused more often will have to pay for representation rather than it being provided by the state. The attorney will also be limited in what they can do during the bench trial. The judge asks the majority of the questions, and the attorney is allowed to ask questions only after the judge has finished asking their questions. Also, the judge is not easily fooled or confused by the evidence or an attorney's skillful representation of the facts in the same way that a jury may be swayed. And in both adversarial and inquisitorial systems, defense attorneys work with prosecutors and judges across many cases. As a result, the defense attorney will be careful not to alienate prosecutors or judges during the process which could mean backing off during a trial when a request on behalf of their client is denied, for example.

Case 8.5: Defense Counsel
Imagine you are a defense attorney advising your client on whether they should spend six months in jail versus joining a drug treatment court that will take between 12 to 18 months to complete. Your client has a job, an apartment, and is addicted to cocaine. If they go to jail they will lose their job and their apartment, but going into the drug treatment program is intensive and may require several months in drug rehab so the client may lose the job and the apartment anyway. Make a list of other factors you and your client should take into consideration when making this decision. After considering the impact of going to jail versus working through a drug treatment court program, what would you recommend to your client?

Ethical Issues for Judges

Judges have broad discretion in both procedure and substance of a case in adversarial systems, but much more so in inquisitorial systems. Judges have personal bias just like any other person and may favor punishment over rehabilitation, for example. Where **judicial discretion** gets the most attention tends to be in sentencing decisions. In one study where sentencing guidelines were used within Maryland, judges were found to sentence African Americans to longer sentences than whites 20% of the time holding age, gender, and sentence length recommended in the sentencing guidelines constant (Bushway & Peihl, 2001). Unfortunately, determining whether racial bias exists in sentencing is difficult given the many factors that influence decisions in sentencing (Baumer, 2013).

Sentencing for judges raises many ethical questions particularly since there is so much judicial discretion in sentencing. Each judge has their own approach, some getting creative with the terms of a sentence particularly in formulating the probation contract. For example, a judge could require a defendant to write a check for $1 every week to the victim (or their family) because of the defendant's drunk driving as a symbolic way to force the defendant to revisit the harm their reckless behavior caused every week. Some jurisdictions including the federal courts have sentencing guidelines that prescribe ranges of punishment based on the severity of the crime and the defendant's previous criminal convictions. Departures from the sentencing guideline ranges are allowed in specific, well-defined circumstances, but the judge has to provide justification for any departure whether it is to be more lenient with the defendant or to give out a harsher punishment.

In the United States, federal judges serve for life and are appointed by the President and confirmed by the Senate. In the states, judges suffer through elections which can be partisan or non-partisan depending on the state. There is a third way to become a judge through a process called merit selection which begins with an appointment process and then the judge later faces a retention election. In an election process, judges are held accountable for their decisions on the bench which can encroach on their judicial independence. This is problematic in that judges are experts and should be able to rely on their legal knowledge and apply it to each case without fear of losing their job should the general voting public disagree with the outcome in a particular case (Pozen, 2008).

In general, all judges can face impeachment, removal from their position, and/or disbarment from the legal profession for professional misconduct. In the United States, the professional rules for attorneys apply to judges, but the judiciary also has its own separate rules of conduct. In criminal trials, judges have a duty to make sure that the defense counsel has had access to exculpatory evidence from the prosecution, that the defense attorney has properly advised their client of all their constitutional rights particularly when plea bargaining, and generally that the defendant has received effective assistance of counsel (Klein, 2006). Where a defendant enters a guilty plea moments after their first consultation with defense counsel then **ineffective assistance of counsel** is assumed (*Bryant v. Peyton*, 1967).

Case 8.6: Judicial Misconduct
U.S. District Judge Aileen Cannon, appointed as a federal judge under President Trump, heard the civil case of *Trump v. United States* regarding the FBI's seizure of classified documents at Trump's residence, Mar-A-Lago. Judge Cannon decided to appoint a special counsel to review the documents and the government appealed her decision which was ultimately overturned. Ethics charges were brought against Judge Cannon asserting that her decision was partisan and not based on any precedent. Whether Judge Cannon acted unethically is a question of law, but whether she should be held accountable for her ruling in Trump's case is a moral question. In other words, should judges be held accountable for decisions they make that are not based on any precedent and, in fact, go against established previous legal decisions?

Conclusion

Regardless of the court system in place, moral dilemmas arise wherever discretion is allowed whether it be prosecutorial, public defender, or judicial. The court system can be transformative, providing support to victims of violence, individuals addicted to illegal substances, and those suffering from mental health issues. The court system can also destroy lives and allow the guilty to go free. Many courts are open to the general public and considering most people have no contact with the criminal justice system this open access can provide the best insight into how courts function day-to-day. If you can't make it down to the courthouse, you can always tune into Court TV which first aired in the early 1990s and is now available streaming live online. Unfortunately, Court TV tends to focus on violent crime and sensational trials which are not the norm within the criminal justice system where non-violent drug crimes and theft are predominant.

Debates for In-Class Discussion

1. The U.S. should switch to an inquisitorial court system
   a. *Pro* – judges are better equipped to resolve legal matters and should have more control over cases than the attorneys who are overburdened with heavy caseloads; inquisitorial systems are more focused on achieving justice
   b. *Con* – a major overhaul of the court system in the U.S. would have severe growing pains and would not prevent corruption and mistakes
2. Criminal courts should adopt a harm reduction strategy for defendants who suffer from addiction
   a. *Pro* – studies show that harm reduction is superior to an abstinence only policy; other countries have adopted a harm reduction approach
   b. *Con* – without some accountability, addicted individuals will not be able to break their cycle of addiction and change behavior

Terms

Model Rules
Lack of communication
Reasonably informed
Informed Consent
Confidentiality
Conflict of interest
Rules of evidence
Diversion courts
Treatment courts
Drug treatment court
Mental health treatment court
Medication-Assisted Treatment (MAT)
Harm reduction
Prosecutorial discretion
Prosecutorial misconduct
Caseloads for public defenders
Ineffective assistance of counsel
Discretion for public defenders
Right to counsel
Duty to represent zealously
Judicial discretion

References

Albonetti, C. A. (1987). Prosecutorial discretion: The effects of uncertainty. *Law and society review*, 291-313.

American Bar Association (ABA). House of Delegates. (2006). Model rules of professional conduct. American Bar Association.

Baker, D. B., & Hassan, S. (2021). Gender and prosecutorial discretion: An empirical assessment. *Journal of Public Administration Research and Theory*, *31*(1), 73-90.

Baldus, D. C., Woodworth, G., & Pulaski, C. A. (1990). *Equal justice and the death penalty: A legal and empirical analysis*. Upne.

Baumer, E. P. (2013). Reassessing and redirecting research on race and sentencing. *Justice Quarterly*, *30*(2), 231-261.

Berger v. United States, 295 U.S. 78 (1935).

Bushway, S. D., & Piehl, A. M. (2001). Judging judicial discretion: Legal factors and racial discrimination in sentencing. *Law and Society Review*, 733-764.

Bryant v. Peyton, 270 F. Supp. 353, 358 (W.D. Va. 1967).

Farole, D. J. & Langton, L. (2010). A national assessment of public defender office caseloads. *Judicature*, *94*(2), 87-90.

Gottlieb, A., & Arnold, K. (2021). The effect of public defender and support staff caseloads on incarceration outcomes for felony defendants. *Journal of the Society for Social Work and Research*, *12*(3), 569-589.

Gross, J. P. (2017). Case Refusal: A Right for the Public Defender but Not a Remedy for the Defendant. *Wash. UL Rev.*, *95*, 253.

Henning, P. J. (1999). Prosecutorial misconduct and constitutional remedies. *Wash. ULQ*, 77(3), 713-834.

Kassin, S. M., Tubb, V. A., Hosch, H. M., & Memon, A. (2001). On the" general acceptance" of eyewitness testimony research: A new survey of the experts. *American Psychologist*, *56*(5), 405.

Klein, R. (2006). Judicial misconduct in criminal cases: It's not just the counsel who may be ineffective and unprofessional. *Ohio St. J. Crim. L.*, *4*, 195.

Linda R. S. v. Richard D., 410 U.S. 614 (1973).

Love, M. C. (2001). The Revised ABA Model Rules of Professional Conduct: Summary of the Work of Ethics 2000. *Geo. J. Legal Ethics*, *15*, 441.

Marlowe, D. B. (2013). Achieving racial and ethnic fairness in drug courts. *Ct. Rev.*, *49*, 40.

Newlyn, D. (2018). Adversarial vs. Inquisitorial legal systems: Rousseau, truth, justice and God. *International Journal of Research in Applied, Natural and Social Sciences*, *6*(5), 165-174.

Pozen, D. E. (2008). The irony of judicial elections. *Columbia Law Review*, 265-330.

Smith, R. J., & Levinson, J. D. (2011). The impact of implicit racial bias on the exercise of prosecutorial discretion. *Seattle UL Rev.*, *35*, 795.

Sorensen, J., & Wallace, D. H. (1999). Prosecutorial discretion in seeking death: An analysis of racial disparity in the pretrial stages of case processing in a Midwestern county. *Justice Quarterly*, *16*(3), 559-578.

Spohn, C., Tellis, K., & O'Neal, E. N. (2014). Policing and prosecuting sexual assault. *Critical issues on violence against women: International perspectives and promising strategies*, 3, 93-103.

State v. Peart, 621 So. 2d 780, 791 (La. 1993).

Tanford, J. A. (2001). The Ethics of Evidence. *Am. J. Trial Advoc.*, *25*, 487.

Chapter 9
Punishment and Corrections

Chapter Objectives

1. Analyze various theories of punishment and the impact each has on defendants, victims, and society.
2. Explore the unique dilemmas faced by individuals supervised under community corrections, as well as incarcerated populations.
3. Discuss moral dilemmas faced by probation, parole, and correctional officers.
4. Consider the value of having a death penalty in modern society and whether it is time for the United States to abolish the ultimate sanction.

Introduction

In 2001, Ted Conover published a book called *Newjack* chronicling a year he spent as a corrections officer in the Ossining correctional facility, more famously known as Sing Sing. Conover captures the myriad of moral dilemmas he faces as he navigates training and later learning how to implement sometimes conflicting rules of his job. The nature of being a correctional officer requires that they rotate different positions throughout the facility which gives insight into every aspect of what it's really like to be a correctional officer.

This chapter focuses on a variety of moral dilemmas within punishment and corrections. With the bail reform movement and rehabilitative approaches within the justice system, jails and prisons, as well as community corrections, have declined somewhat, but remain robust overall (Carson & Kluckow, 2023). Probation officers have transitioned from purely criminal justice roles to more rehabilitative, social work-related roles in changing offenders' lives. Similarly, parole officers are also engaged heavily in social work and rehabilitation, helping offenders find jobs, stable housing, and counseling services when returning to the community. And corrections officers typically face understaffing within their facilities, strained relationships with inmates, and role conflict. This chapter addresses the issues that arise in modern-day correctional environments as a result of trends in punishment theory.

Punishment

Punishment serves a multitude of purposes in the justice system including retribution, incapacitation, deterrence, rehabilitation, and restorative justice. Each of the five main theoretical purposes for punishment has its pros and cons. In the United States, the focus has been to reduce jail and prison populations which has steered punishment policy away from retribution and incapacitation and towards rehabilitative and restorative practices. While the focus may be on rehabilitation and restorative justice within the justice system, each theory of punishment still thrives within the justice system depending on the jurisdiction and the people working within the system. Unfortunately, accurately measuring the impact of initiatives designed to reduce incarcerated populations have been interrupted by the pandemic where large numbers of individuals were released from correctional institutions to control the spread of COVID.

Retribution at its most basic level is the concept of a harm for a harm (Kelln and Ellard, 1999). The goal of **retribution** then as punishment is to punish someone who commits a crime with a punishment that fits the crime and no other factors. According to Kant, the punishment fitting the crime is important towards achieving the goals of the state in protecting society while simultaneously providing fairness in sentencing (Kant, 2017). Generally, though, retribution is equated with the concept of harsh punishment in terms of longer sentences and higher incarceration rates (Flanders, 2010). Retribution is often mentioned in tandem with deterrence theory suggesting that if the punishment fits the crime, then perhaps the goal of deterrence will be achieved at least with respect to the individual committing the crime.

We think of **deterrence** as either punishment aimed at deterring the future crime of individuals - **specific deterrence** - or punishment aimed at deterring others within society from committing future crimes - **general deterrence**. Kant was a strong proponent of deterrence theory, as well, focusing on **general deterrence** as a primary goal of punishment (Kant, 2017). Deterrence theory receives mixed results in terms of practical application within a variety of contexts. In order for **deterrence** to be effective, the punishment must be swift, certain, and severe enough to cause behavioral changes. And individual characteristics of the offender are critical in determining effectiveness of sanctions in deterring criminal behaviors. Some individual characteristics that influence deterrence from crime include:

1. Social bonds an individual has to family, friends, and employment;
2. An individual's moral inhibition and personal commitment to following rules;
3. Self-control, impulsivity, and discounting of consequences for criminal behavior;
4. Emotional and pharmacological influences;
5. Position within a social network;
6. Level of decision-making competency (Piquero et al., 2011)

Incapacitation gets very little attention in terms of a theory of punishment but is important in terms of providing a short-term solution to stopping criminal behavior in the moment. It is a mechanism for separating someone engaged in criminal behavior from society through detention typically and can often be studied alongside **deterrence** since the strategies are similar – incarcerate as a means to deter crime. **Incapacitation** theory provides that the more people who are incarcerated for committing crimes, the lower the crime rate since the people who would be committing crimes are incapacitated in correctional facilities. However, studies have shown that **incapacitation** as a long-term strategy for reducing the crime rate is not effective (Donziger, 1996).

These three theories of **punishment** predominated the correctional landscape in the United States during both the Nixon and Reagan presidencies. Political rhetoric focused on establishing **"get tough" policies** with respect to violent crimes and drug related offenses. As a result, large numbers of young, black and Hispanic youth were targeted resulting in a mass incarceration epidemic in the United States. This shift in **punishment** policy was seen as backlash from the Civil Rights movement and more rehabilitative approaches under both Kennedy and Johnson administrations (Harty, 2012). Current **punishment** policy appears to be gravitating back towards a rehabilitative approach.

Rehabilitation is a theory of **punishment** that is very unlike its counterparts. Rather than focusing on sanctions, **rehabilitation** focuses on providing resources to those committing crimes in order to change attitudes and behaviors. **Rehabilitation** usually includes mental health treatment, substance abuse treatment, job and housing assistance, life skills training, access to education and job skills training, as well as access to health care and basic living necessities. Rehabilitative services are usually less expensive than incarceration and decrease recidivism rates. Diversion or treatment courts are one example of a rehabilitative approach within the justice system as is discussed in the previous chapter on the court system.

Restorative Justice, as discussed in Chapter 5 of this text, focuses on restoring the victim, their family, and society from the harm caused by the crime committed against them. Like rehabilitation, it is significantly different than other theories of punishment which all focus on the offender. Restorative Justice is growing rapidly across college campuses which makes sense given the nature of college disciplinary infractions. **Restorative Justice** is being tested in some college and community jurisdictions and is seeing preliminary positive outcomes with victims of sexual assault.

Case 9.1: Theories of Punishment
Consider the systems of ethics explored in Chapter 2 (religion, natural law, Utilitarianism, Ethics of Care, Ethical Egoism, and Ethical Formalism). With the following examples, which theory of punishment best serves the defendant, the victim(s), and/or society within the context of the ethical systems discussed in Chapter 2? 1. Carla, a victim of human trafficking, has been arrested for prostitution. She came to the United States with the promise of work to pay off her debt for travel expenses from her home country. Upon arrival, her passport was confiscated by her trafficker, and she was threatened with violence should she try to leave. Carla does not speak much English, so she did not seek help. 2. John is addicted to cocaine. He has been through rehab before but has relapsed and was recently picked up on larceny charges when he was caught stealing in order to feed his addiction. He does not have any violent offenses on his record but has several misdemeanor charges of theft and shoplifting as well as criminal possession.

Community Corrections

Now more than ever the vast majority of individuals caught up in the criminal justice system are involved in **community corrections** supervised by **probation** and **parole officers** with the majority of that **population** on **probation** (Carson & Kluckow, 2023). Historically, **probation** focused on making recommendations for sentencing and managing those under their supervision. The same holds true today, however, with some significant shifts in approach. In both sentencing recommendations and managing caseloads, the pendulum of **probation** policy has swung away from a harsh, "get tough" approach towards a more lenient, rehabilitative approach. Rather than charging someone under their supervision with a violation of **probation** for every infraction, for example, there is a focus on reconnecting individuals to support services in order to keep them out of jail and prison.

Population Type	2011		2022	
	Total Population	*% of Population*	*Total Population*	*% of Population*
Total	6,994,500	100%	5,444,900	100%
Probation	3,973,800	56.8%	2,963,000	54.4%
Prison	1,599,000	22.9%	1,204,300	22.1%
Parole	855,500	12.2%	803,200	14.8%
Local jail	735,600	10.5%	636,300	11.7%

Table 9.1: *U.S. Correctional Status: 2011 Compared to 2021*
*numbers are approximate due to nonresponse, rounding, and excluding dual correctional status
*(Carson & Kluckow, 2023)

Probation officers have some discretion in making sentencing recommendations, however, their recommendations tend to align with the judge they are working with to avoid conflict. Sentencing recommendations are also heavily dependent on the defendant's current charges and past convictions. Even with these constraints the probation officer still has some influence in terms of how to present recommendations to the judge.

The shift in **punishment** policy from harsher punishment to **rehabilitation** makes sense given that individuals on **probation** tend to have higher rates of medical problems without access to affordable health insurance and increased rates of substance abuse, as well as mental health issues. In terms of probation racial demographics both young black males and Hispanics who have only lower levels of education are at the greatest risk of becoming involved in **probation** (Phelps, 2020). This is not surprising given the **"get tough" policies** that targeted young, black and brown men (Alexander, 2020).

Meanwhile, **parole** has two main objectives which include preparing individuals for reentry into society upon completion of their imprisonment and, like **probation**, supervising those on **parole**. Jobs and housing are the primary goals of reentry, but also other support services aimed at keeping individuals from recidivating. Finding employers and landlords who will accept individuals with a conviction is challenging. Conditions of **probation** and **parole** typically include **probation/parole officers** conducting check-ins with their clients both at home and at work. Even where the employer or the landlord may be comfortable with this arrangement, often co-workers and neighbors are not.

The role of **probation and parole officers** has shifted over time to take on more of the role of a social worker with respect to their supervision of clients under their watch. Keeping clients engaged in job training, work, counseling therapy, substance abuse treatment, finding stable housing, and generally taking care of themselves is essentially the kind of work that social workers engage in – a type of case management. In the United States, there is no formal training or licensure specifically for becoming a probation and/or parole officer, however, in the United Kingdom there has historically been both educational degree programs and licensure depending on the political party in power (Annison et al., 2008).

Case 9.2: Probation Recommendations

Imagine that you're a probation officer who is making a recommendation to a judge in the following cases:

1. A repeat non-violent offender who has a history of homelessness and vagrancy in the community, generally for being a nuisance and upsetting local business owners
2. A young mother who has an opioid addiction
3. A young man who has threatened his girlfriend with violence on repeated occasions

What impact does any of the following have on your recommendations:

1. the judge's sentencing style (a judge who leans towards rehabilitation versus a judge who leans towards harsher sentences)
2. prior non-violent and prior violent convictions
3. whether the defendant has kids living at home
4. the age of the defendant

Case 9.3: Probation Violations

As a condition of probation/parole, typically individuals have constraints on who they can spend time with including convicted felons or maybe someone who has enabled them in abusing substances. Imagine you are a probation/parole officer and over the weekend when you are at the movies with your family, you see one of your clients with someone they shouldn't be with. What are your options in responding to this? What factors would you consider important in making your decision for a course of action? If the client has children that could potentially end up in foster care should their probation be revoked, what impact would this have on your decision to report the potential infraction?

Correctional Institutions and Officers

Incarceration historically was developed to replace harsher forms of punishment like whipping and beating. The penitentiary was the result;

however, **incarceration** was initially a very isolating and harsh environment. Architectural designs of correctional institutions have evolved over time to become less isolating incorporating practical spaces for educational and vocational programming, as well as spaces that promote overall physical and mental health.

According to Michelle Alexander (2020), incarceration is the new Jim Crow of our time evidenced by the disproportionate numbers of black inmates found in the United States correctional system. For example, in 2021, black populations in correctional facilities were at about 31% while their census numbers in 2020 were at around 12% in the general population (Carson & Kluckow, 2023; Census, 2020). Public policy, policing tactics, legal constraints, and implicit bias have each contributed to a **racial caste system** of mass incarceration that is unprecedented (Alexander, 2020).

Race	2011		2022	
	Total Population	*% of Population*	*Total Population*	*% of Population*
Total	2,252,000	100%	1,775,000	100%
White	803,000	35.7%	658,000	37.1%
Black	823,000	36.5%	591,000	33.3%
Hispanic	450,000	20.0%	359,000	20.2%
Other	176,000	7.8%	167,000	9.4%

Table 9.2: *Prison and Jail Populations by Race 2011 Compared to 2021*
*numbers are approximate due to nonresponse, rounding, and excluding dual correctional status
*(Carson & Kluckow, 2023)

Some of the biggest problems that correctional institutions face includes physical and mental health care for incarcerated individuals. Harsh sentencing has led to aging prison populations where health care needs steadily increase. The COVID-19 pandemic placed even greater strains on correctional institutions to protect their populations forcing many institutions to release large numbers of their residents early (Franco-Paredes et al., 2021). And suicide rates for inmates range from 3 to 10 times higher in prison populations as compared to the general population depending on a number of factors (Zhong et al., 2021). Correctional institutions owe a duty to provide a certain level of care for those under their supervision as sentences for **incarceration** should not end up being death sentences.

Programming in jails and prisons has greatly expanded over the last several decades to include opportunities for education, training, and self-improvement. Generally, there are five types of evidence-based programming found in prisons:

1. Substance abuse and mental health treatment both residential and non-residential
2. Educational and vocational training
3. Work and employment
4. Mentoring and social support
   (Byrne, 2020)

Whether these programs reduce recidivism varies, however, many programs have received widespread attention for their success including the Bard Prison Initiative (BPI) bringing higher education into prisons, mindfulness practices like mediation and yoga, and the Puppies Behind Bars (PBB) program where incarcerated individuals train service and bomb sniffing dogs.

In-house work programs have garnered some criticism for under-paying incarcerated individuals. This is not a new phenomenon as prison chain gangs and incarcerated slave labor has its foundations in American history. In 2016, prisoners went on strike demanding better pay (Kim, 2016). State prisoners earn between $0.93 to $4.73 per hour and federal prisoners earn anywhere from $0.00 to $4.73 per *day* while private prisons have the lowest pay of $0.16 to $0.50 per hour (Fulcher, 2013). In December 2023, a group of both current and former Alabama incarcerated individuals filed a lawsuit against the state for forcing them to work in exchange for little to no pay calling the prison labor program "modern day slavery" (Levenson, 2023).

Correctional officers face a variety of challenges many of which are identified in Conover's book mentioned at the beginning of this chapter. Dangerous work conditions, understaffing, unpleasant work environments, and facing stressful situations are just a part of their work experience day-to-day. Conover stresses that the biggest challenge is cultivating healthy relationships within the correctional environment whether that be relationships among correctional staff, among incarcerated individuals, or between incarcerated individuals and correctional staff. Both incarcerated individuals and correctional staff can take advantage of one another if given the opportunity.

Private prisons make up only a small portion of correctional facilities in the United States. Research on whether privatization of correctional facilities is more effective and/or efficient shows mixed results (Gaes, 2019). Some studies find modest cost savings with private prisons, some find better reductions in recidivism with traditional prisons, and others find better environmental conditions in private prisons. Morally, however, it is hard to justify a private facility making a profit from the punishment and incarceration of human beings.

Case 9.4: The New Jim Crow
A **racial caste system** is one where groups in society are hierarchical with each group having different levels of superiority and there is always at least one group that is seen as inferior to the others. Much of society then revolves around this caste system – giving societal benefits to some and not others like jobs and social status. Several scholars have argued that people live in caste systems in the United States, and caste systems have been recognized in other countries like India. Laws, customs, institutions, and society all work to support the caste system. Michelle Alexander's argument is that there is a **racial caste system** in the United States, and it is exemplified by mass incarceration as a replacement for the elimination of Jim Crow laws. What do you think of this argument? If Alexander is correct, what can be done about this?

Case 9.5: Prison Wages for Incarcerated Individuals
What should the rate of pay be for incarcerated individuals? Large companies like Victoria's Secret benefit from their labor avoiding shipping jobs overseas to other countries. It also allows for a "Made in America" stamp on their products. Is it an exploitation of workers who are incarcerated or is it an opportunity for them to get job experience and prepare for reentry back into society? What factors should be considered in determining the rate of pay for incarcerated individuals?

Case 9.6: Private Prisons
In 2021, the federal government through Presidential Executive Order decided to end reliance on private prisons within the federal system leaving it up to individual states as to whether they will use them within their jurisdictions. Should we rely on private prisons? What factors would you consider in making this decision? How would you weigh factors like efficiency and effectiveness of these institutions? Under what conditions would you want to keep them and under what conditions would you want to eliminate them?

Death Penalty

Every society in the world at one time or another has had a **death penalty** of some sorts whether it is headhunting, putting someone in a canoe and pushing them out to sea with little to no supplies, crucifixion, or lethal injection. The **death penalty** has been around at least since the 18th century BC and in some societies was the only punishment no matter what the crime. The death penalty came to the United States with the original settlers and was relied on for a variety of both religious and secular crimes including denying God and stealing (Randa, 1997).

Arguments in support of the **death penalty** include providing closure for victims and/or their families, as a deterrent to future crime, and retribution for the crime committed. However, studies have shown that the death penalty is not a deterrent to crime (Parker, 2021). Society appears to be moving away from the death penalty. In a recent Gallop Poll (2019), 60% of respondents favored life without parole over the death penalty in murder cases as compared to 59% who favored the death penalty in 1993. Membership in the European Union requires that member countries abolish their death penalty. According to the Death Penalty Information Center (DPIC), as of December 2022, there are 144 countries that have abolished the **death penalty** as opposed to 55 countries that have retained it.

Country	Number of executions
China	1,000s*
Iran	576+*
Saudi Arabia	196
Egypt	24
USA	18
Iraq	11+*
Singapore	11
Kuwait	7
Somalia	6+

Table 9.3: *Countries with the Highest Number of Confirmed Executions in 2022*
*Exact totals unknown
(DPIC, 2022a)

In 1972 in the United States, there was a brief moratorium placed on executions as a result of ***Furman v. Georgia***. In a split decision, the Court found the death penalty was "freakish" in its application making it discriminatory against black defendants. In response, prosecutors and state legislatures changed the administration of the death penalty in two ways. First, they added a separate penalty phase post-conviction. And second, they established mitigating and aggravating circumstances for determining whether a case is death penalty eligible. Four years later, in ***Gregg v. Georgia,*** the U.S. Supreme Court overturned the *Furman* case in a 7 to 2 decision.

Since the reinstatement of the **death penalty** in the United States there have been 1,578 executions according to the Death Penalty Information Center. Recently, however, there has been a sharp decline as only six states executed prisoners in 2022. The leader by far in executions has always been Texas which has also declined steadily from the height of its executions in 2000 with 40 prisoners executed down to 5 prisoners in 2022.

State	Total executions since 1976	2023	2022	2021
Texas	584	6	5	3
Oklahoma	122	3	5	2
Florida	105	6	0	0
Missouri	97	4	2	1
Alabama	71	1	2	1
Arizona	40	0	3	0
Mississippi	23	0	1	1

Table 9.4: *States Who Continue to Execute Prisoners* (DPIC, 2023)

Unfortunately, the changes made did not prevent racial discrimination in **death penalty** cases. Race of both the defendant and victim greatly impacts whether a defendant will receive the **death penalty** (DPIC, 2022b). Other problems with administering the **death penalty** include errors in the system. Faulty eyewitness testimony, false confessions, ineffective assistance of counsel, faulty evidence collection and/or analysis, and prosecutorial misconduct account for hundreds of mistakes made according to the Innocence Project.

In 1999, students at Northwestern University working on a class project found exonerating evidence in the Anthony Porter case. This prompted the Chicago Tribune to investigate a couple dozen random cases that were on death row at the time. What they found was that half of the cases they investigated were factually innocent of the charges against them. All of this caught the attention of then Illinois Governor George Ryan, a Republican and staunch supporter of the death penalty. Ryan decided to put a commission together to look into it and eventually authorized extensive hearings for every convicted prisoner on death row. Ryan also happened to be at the end of his term as Governor, having not sought re-election. His decision-making process and the entire event are captured in a documentary called *Deadline*.

Since Governor Ryan's reconsideration of the death penalty, many states decided to place moratoriums on their death penalties citing errors in the justice process as well as discrimination. In 23 states and the District of Columbia, the death penalty has been abolished as of December 2023. While the remaining 27 states still have the death penalty, 5 of those states have Governors that have put a hold on executions within their states. Of the remaining states, most have not held an execution in years (DPIC, 2023).

The U.S. Supreme Court has found the death penalty to violate the **Eighth Amendment's cruel and unusual standard** in cases where the defendant is under the age of 18 in ***Roper v. Simmons*** or has a low IQ in ***Atkins v. Virginia***. They have also found that the death penalty is not appropriate in non-murder cases in ***Coker v. Georgia*** and ***Kennedy v. Louisiana***. Challenges to methods of execution have not been successful, however, states ran into problems when suppliers for the drugs used in lethal injections refused to continue selling their products for the use of administering the death penalty. Some states have begun finding alternate sources for their lethal injection drugs, but another dilemma has been finding healthcare providers who are willing to administer the injections, particularly doctors who have a Hippocratic Oath to do no harm and some states require licensed physicians to oversee executions.

Case 9.7: Administering the Death Penalty
As a warden for a prison in a state that still executes prisoners, what do you do if faced with an inmate whose innocence is still in question? How do you choose staff to oversee the execution? And how do you prepare someone for working an execution as a staff member within a prison? What about if you were a staff member – would you feel any differently? How would you prepare for working an execution? And, what about the death row chaplain? How do you prepare someone for execution? How do you prepare yourself?

Case 9.8: Governor Ryan's Decision
Imagine you are a Governor, and you discover that most likely half of your prisoners on death row may have been wrongfully convicted. What approach would you take to make a decision about what to do in your state? What information do you need to know in order to make that decision? What impact will your personal feelings about the death penalty have on your decision-making? Consider the systems of ethics explored in Chapter 2 (religion, natural law, Utilitarianism, Ethics of Care, Ethical Egoism, and Ethical Formalism). Applying these theories discussed in Chapter 2 to the death penalty, which ethical system best serves the defendant, the victim(s), and/or society?

Conclusion

Punishment is often seen as a mechanism for changing behavior whether it is used as a deterrent, rehabilitation, or a way to restore victims. Changing behavior, however, is extremely challenging as anyone who has tried to change the behavior of a family member, friend, or even a puppy will attest to. Rewards typically go further than sanctions when trying to change behavior whether it be human or canine and the correctional system is not particularly focused on incentives. And yet the term "corrections" implies positive change in terms of fixing a mistake. This chapter has raised many moral dilemmas faced within the correctional system that are not easily resolved, but there is hope through the use of specialized probation programs, diversion courts, innovative prison programs, and aggressive reentry strategies.

Debate Topics for In-Class Discussion

1. Probation/Parole officers should have a specialized degree
   a. *Pro* – advanced education will create a more professional workforce and could lead to better outcomes for individuals who are on probation/parole
   b. *Con* – it's challenging to find college graduates who want to go into corrections – more so than policing - which would then severely limit hiring pools
2. It is time to end the death penalty in the United States
   a. *Pro* – there is no deterrence benefit from having a death penalty, it is racist as applied, having a death penalty is too costly, most countries have abolished it, and morally it is wrong for the state to sanction murder
   b. *Con* – there has been a death penalty of some type in virtually every society at one point or another in time, victims' families need closure, it is generally supported by prosecutors and citizens

Terms

Punishment
Retribution
Deterrence
Specific deterrence
General deterrence
Incapacitation
"Get tough" policies
Rehabilitation
Restorative Justice
Community corrections
Probation
Parole
Probation officers
Parole officers
Incarceration
Private prisons
Death penalty
Furman v. Georgia
Gregg v. Georgia
Eighth Amendment Cruel and Unusual
Roper v. Simmons
Atkins v. Virginia
Coker v. Georgia
Kennedy v. Louisiana
Racial caste system

References

Alexander, M. (2020). *The new Jim Crow: Mass incarceration in the age of colorblindness*. The New Press.

Annison, J., Eadie, T., & Knight, C. (2008). People first: Probation officer perspectives on probation work. *Probation Journal, 55*(3), 259-271.

Atkins v. Virginia, 536 U.S. 304 (2002).

Byrne, J. M. (2020). The effectiveness of prison programming: A review of the research literature examining the impact of federal, state, and local inmate programming on post-release recidivism. *Fed. Probation, 84,* 3.

Carson, E., & Kluckow, R. (2023). Correctional populations in the United States, 2021–Statistical tables. Office of Justice Programs. Bureau of Justice Statistics.

Census. (2020). Quick Facts United States Population.

Coker v. Georgia, 433 U.S. 584 (1977).

Death Penalty Information Center (DPIC). (2022a). *Abolitionist and Retentionist Countries.* https://deathpenaltyinfo.org/policy-issues/international/abolitionist-and-retentionist-countries

Death Penalty Information Center (DPIC). (2022b). *Executions by Race and Race of Victim.* https://deathpenaltyinfo.org/executions/executions-overview/executions-by-race-and-race-of-victim

Death Penalty Information Center (DPIC). (2023). *State by State.* https://deathpenaltyinfo.org/states-landing

Donziger, S. (1996). *The real war on crime: The report of the National Criminal Justice Commission*. New York: Harper Perennial.

Flanders, C. (2010). Retribution and Reform. *Md. L. Rev., 70,* 87.

Franco-Paredes, C., Ghandnoosh, N., Latif, H., Krsak, M., Henao-Martinez, A. F., Robins, M., Vargas Barahona, L., & Poeschla, E. M. (2021). Decarceration and community re-entry in the COVID-19 era. *The Lancet. Infectious diseases, 21*(1), e11–e16.

Fulcher, P. A. (2013). Emancipate the FLSA: Transform the harsh economic reality of working inmates. *JCR & Econ. Dev., 27,* 679.

Furman v. Georgia, 408 U.S. 23 (1972).

Gaes, G. G. (2019). Current status of prison privatization research on American prisons and jails. *Criminology & Public Policy, 18*(2), 269-293.

Gallop. (2019). *Death Penalty*. https://news.gallup.com/poll/1606/death-penalty.aspx

Gregg v. Georgia, 428 U.S. 153 (1976).

Harty, C. M. (2012). The causes and effects of get tough: A look at how tough-on-crime policies rose to the agenda and an examination of their effects on prison populations and crime.

Kant, I. (2017). *Kant: The metaphysics of morals*. Cambridge University Press.

Kelln, B. R., & Ellard, J. H. (1999). An equity theory analysis of the impact of forgiveness and retribution on transgressor compliance. *Personality and Social Psychology Bulletin, 25*(7), 864-872.

Kennedy v. Louisiana, 554 U.S. 407 (2008).

Kim, T. (2016). A national strike against 'prison slavery'. *The New Yorker*.

Levenson, M. (2023, Dec. 12). Prisoners Sue Alabama, Calling Prison Labor System a 'Form of Slavery'. *The New York Times*.

Parker, B. (2021). Death penalty statutes and murder rates: Evidence from synthetic controls. *Journal of Empirical Legal Studies, 18*(3), 488-533.

Phelps, M. S. (2020). Mass probation from micro to macro: Tracing the expansion and consequences of community supervision. *Annual Review of Criminology*, 3, 261-279

Piquero, A. R., Paternoster, R., Pogarsky, G., & Loughran, T. (2011). Elaborating the individual difference component in deterrence theory. *Annual Review of Law and Social Science, 7*, 335-360.

Randa, L. E. (1997). Society's final solution: A history and discussion of the death penalty.

Roper v. Simmons, 543 U.S. 551 (2005).

Zhong, S., Senior, M., Yu, R., Perry, A., Hawton, K., Shaw, J., & Fazel, S. (2021). Risk factors for suicide in prisons: a systematic review and meta-analysis. *The Lancet Public Health, 6*(3), e164-e174.

Chapter 10
Humanitarian Law

Chapter Objectives

1. Expose students to the concept of International Humanitarian Law and the impact it has on protecting society.
2. Discuss violations of International Humanitarian Law and how those cases are handled by the United Nations and the International Criminal Court.
3. Consider the impact that genocide, crimes against humanity, war crimes, and crimes of aggression have on society.
4. Compare historical cases of moral dilemmas that arise as a result of violations of International Humanitarian Law.

Introduction

Imagine you are a soldier in the military sent to the middle east to guard suspected terrorists in Iraq. While guarding the prisoners, your commanding officer asks you to help interrogate some of the prisoners. As part of the interrogation, you must strip them naked, put pillowcases over their heads, and drag them across the floor to intimidate them into talking. This is what happened in Abu Ghraib with American soldiers who were told to use questionable tactics in order to garner intelligence from detainees being held in the prison. The Abu Ghraib scandal involved everyday street-level bureaucrats forced to make moral decisions that ended up costing lives. The Abu Ghraib scandal is the subject of a documentary called *Ghosts of Abu Ghraib* (2007).

The United States violated **International Humanitarian Law (IHL)** in their treatment of prisoners at the Abu Ghraib prison. But what are the real consequences in a situation like this? Keeping countries in compliance with **IHL** is a challenging task but there are laws and institutions that work to hold countries accountable when they are not in compliance. Chapter 10 provides an in-depth look at humanitarian law, the Geneva Conventions, the Just War Tradition, enhanced interrogation techniques, torture, and the International Criminal Court (ICC).

Humanitarian Law and the Geneva Conventions

Humanitarian law consists primarily of the **Geneva Conventions** and its Additional Protocols. The first **Geneva Conventions** were written in 1864 and were greatly expanded in 1949 and there have been three Additional Protocols added since then. The first two protocols were added in 1977 and a third protocol was added in 2005. All nations participate in the **Geneva Conventions** but not all support the Additional Protocols. Countries engaged in armed conflict must adhere to the **Geneva Conventions** regarding the treatment of people during any type of armed conflict and the conventions provide protections for those who are engaged in the conflict, as well as those who are not engaged in the conflict.

The **Geneva Conventions** identify lawful enemy combatants and unlawful enemy combatants based on whether the members of militia wear distinctive signs and openly carry their arms, as well as whether they follow the rules of warfare. Prisoners of war are also defined and given specific protections including access to food, medical care, correspondence with family members, and accommodations, as well as protection against violence. There are also protections regarding informing family members when a family member has died during the conflict, the management of human remains, and the return of human remains to their families.

Protocol II of the **Geneva Conventions** also specifies certain acts that are always prohibited. These acts include murder, torture, corporal punishment, mutilation, taking hostages, execution without a trial, cruel and degrading treatment, as well as outrages upon personal dignity. In the Abu Ghraib prison scandal, for example, cruel and degrading treatment and outrages upon personal dignity clearly occurred, as well as various interrogation techniques that the U.S. government characterizes as **enhanced interrogation** but have been identified as **torture** by human rights organizations.

The **International Committee of the Red Cross (ICRC)** is an independent organization recognized worldwide as the entity engaged in promoting **IHL** and the Geneva Conventions. Founded in 1863, the **ICRC** receives funding voluntarily from countries around the world. The **ICRC** deploys to areas of armed conflict and promotes a wide range of services including helping detainees, caring for those injured or killed during the armed conflict, ensuring educational services for children, providing aid to refugees, mitigating the use of mines during warfare, facilitating diplomacy, addressing sexual violence, and helping to ensure basic necessities are met.

When a violation of **IHL** occurs, then the **ICRC** and other nations can put pressure on the nation that is in violation to use their domestic laws to prosecute individuals responsible for the **IHL** violation. In the Abu Ghraib case, the United States asserted that the abuses that happened were the result of a few soldiers who were acting on their own rather than at the direction of the U.S. government. This assertion has been widely disputed by the **ICRC** and several other **IHL** organizations like Amnesty International (Smeulers & Van Niekerk, 2009). The U.S. responded by convicting about a dozen soldiers with mostly minor offenses like dereliction of duty despite the fact that 36 detainees died while in custody as a result of natural causes, mortar blasts, and some were for unknown causes. One senior officer was demoted; however, five other high-ranking officials were either cleared of all wrongdoing and/or given prestigious assignments.

Case 10.1: International Humanitarian Law
On October 7, 2023, a terrorist organization, Hamas, launched a large-scale surprise attack on civilians in Israel. Over 1,400 people in Israel were killed with over 4,500 injured and over 200 hostages were taken by Hamas and held captive in tunnels in the Palestinian controlled Gaza strip (Hutchinson, 2023). Israel announced that it would retaliate and ordered everyone living in Gaza to leave creating a large-scale humanitarian nightmare by displacing and creating thousands of refugees. Humanitarian aid to the area was largely disrupted, causing problems for innocent civilians living there and causing some hospitals to shut down entirely. IHL recognizes the need for nations to respond with force when they are attacked, however, response invariably causes human rights violations. Should Israel have held off on attacking right away and sought diplomatic resolutions for the recovery of their citizens? Much of the humanitarian aid was halted to the area for fear of Hamas getting control over some of that aid, giving them more power to continue. What impact should this fear that Hamas will steal supplies have on the flow of aid to the area?

Just War Theory/Tradition

Killing is considered immoral under most religions and moral doctrines. As with everything in life, there are exceptions. Self-defense and the defense of others are notable exceptions to committing a murder. If someone is attacking you, then you are justified in defending yourself even if the result is death for the attacker. There are some limitations in that the use of force used in self-defense must be reasonable under the circumstances and the non-aggressor has a duty to retreat.

The **Just War Theory**, also known as the **Just War Tradition**, is an extension of self-defense and the defense of others. Under prescribed criteria, it can be considered moral to engage in armed conflict. For example, Russia attacking Ukraine in 2022 was not supported by the **Just War Theory** because Russia was an unprovoked aggressor in that armed conflict. Russia would have had to meet the criteria required under the **Just War Theory** for their invasion to be considered moral.

However, Ukraine defending its citizens is considered acceptable moral behavior. Once attacked, Ukraine can also launch initiatives to try and bring an end to the armed conflict.

Just War Theory has evolved over hundreds of years and has roots in religion being guided historically by legal scholars, philosophers, and theologians (Crawford, 2003). There are two main components of **Just War Theory** which include **jus ad bellum** and **jus in bello**. **Jus ad bellum** establishes whether there is a right to go to war and **jus in bello** dictates the conduct allowed within a war. In order to engage in armed conflict that is justified, a nation state must adhere to both components.

The right to go to war, **jus ad bellum**, exists if a competent or legitimate authority – typically the sovereignty of a state - has a just cause. In addition to self-defense, preemptive strikes where there is a credible threat are also acceptable or to restore peace and status quo to a region (Crawford, 2003). War must be a last resort when all diplomacy has been exhausted and there must be a reasonable hope of success. The amount of force should begin proportionally small, increasing over time only as necessary to end the conflict (Childress, 1978).

Once conflict has begun under **jus in bello** the conduct within the war requires obligations of avoiding causing injuries to human life and unnecessary suffering as much as is possible (Childress, 1978). According to Kant, some behaviors – assassination, the use of poison, not accepting surrender, and encouraging treason within the opposing nation state - even in war should be avoided as these may impede the potential for achieving peace between conflicting nations (Humphrey, 1983).

While self-defense of life is well-accepted in society, there are other things we value worth protecting through use of force. For example, access to life's necessities like food or water and, generally speaking, freedom. Deciding which values are worth protecting with physical force, however, is trickier as is establishing how much evidence is needed to show that force is necessary in protecting what we value. Likewise, establishing that all other possible resolutions have been exhausted before resorting to the use of violence may be difficult. And there is the problem that everyone, terrorists and extremists included, believes their use of force and/or war is a just cause making determining whether an armed conflict is necessary challenging, at best (Crawford, 2003).

Case 10.2: Russia's basis for war
Vladimir Putin claims that Ukraine was militarized, full of Nazis, and was engaged in genocide. Each of these claims is false, but Russia invaded Ukraine in February 2022 nonetheless. Which parts of the Just War Theory did Russia violate? What duty does the rest of the world owe Ukraine or any other country wrongfully invaded and violating the Just War Tradition?

Case 10.3: Assassination
Between 1943 and 1944, there were several plots to assassinate Hitler, but each was discovered as well as a related coup to overthrow the Nazi regime. Are these actions justified under the Just War Theory/Tradition? What would Kant have to say about the assassination attempts? Would Kant feel any differently about a coup?

Torture and Enhanced Interrogation

President George W. Bush (Jr.) set policies post 9/11 referred to as **enhanced interrogation** that allowed psychological and physical interrogation techniques that included stress positions, waterboarding, sensory deprivation, sleep deprivation, loud or deafening music, sexual humiliation, and exposure to extreme heat or cold. Stress positions are those physical positions where most of an individual's body weight is placed on one or two muscles for a lengthy amount of time which first causes muscle fatigue but can eventually lead to muscle failure. Waterboarding is a simulated drowning where the victim has their airway covered in either a soaked cloth of water or their head in a bucket of water while being punched in the stomach to force breathing water into the lungs. Sensory deprivation typically involves putting a hood over someone's head.

These **enhanced interrogation** techniques were established via a Presidential directive to the CIA in 2001 combined with a series of memos from the Justice Department that are commonly referred to as the **Torture Memos**. One criticism of these policies is that they were set by people who have never endured similar pain and thus do not have the same level of empathy as someone who is subjected to the interrogation techniques in question (Nordgren et al., 2011). Another criticism of **enhanced interrogation** is that it is **torture**. In 2009, President Obama revoked Bush's authorization of **enhanced interrogation** and banned the use of those techniques.

The United Nations (UN) and the **Geneva Conventions** both outline what actions constitute torture. The **Geneva Conventions** prohibit **torture** which it defines as:

> . . . any act by which severe pain or suffering, whether physical or mental, is intentionally inflicted on a person for such purposes as obtaining from him or a third person information or a confession, punishing him for an act he or a third person has committed or is suspected of having committed, or intimidating or coercing him or a third person, or for any reason based on discrimination of any kind, when such pain or suffering is inflicted by or at the instigation of or with the consent or acquiescence of a public official or other person acting in an official capacity. It does not include pain or suffering arising only from, inherent in, or incidental to, lawful sanctions. (Article 1.1)

Widespread acts of **torture** committed against a civilian population are considered a **crime against humanity** and **torture** committed during armed conflict is considered a war crime. Both instances fall under the jurisdiction of the **ICC**.

One additional criticism of **enhanced interrogation** is that it may not yield accurate intelligence. Under duress, people will say just about anything to end the pain. Politicians and scholars disagree as to whether any reliable intelligence came from the use of enhanced interrogation by the CIA post 9/11. According to the Carr Center for Human Rights Policy at the Harvard Kennedy School, relying on torture damaged U.S. national security, incited extremism, and undermined U.S. diplomacy (Johnson et al., 2016).

Another problem with intelligence gathered through interrogation generally is that it is very time consuming. In order to extract information from questioning the interviews can take place over many days, weeks, and even months rendering the results outdated by the time the intelligence is gathered. Yet another criticism is the damage to a country's foreign relations reputation where these techniques are condoned. And countries who rely on **enhanced interrogation** are simply giving terrorist organizations a recruitment tool and increasing the membership of terrorist groups.

Case 10.4: Enhanced interrogation/torture
Murat Kurnaz is a citizen of Turkey who lives in Germany who was arrested while traveling through Pakistan a few months after 9/11. He was questioned by local police who sold him to the American military claiming that Kurnaz was a terrorist despite no evidence to support their claim. Kurnaz wrote a book that details how he was tortured at a military base in Afghanistan by U.S. soldiers before being sent to Guantanamo Bay, Cuba where he was further tortured and wrongfully detained for five years. Kurnaz's account includes descriptions of beatings, sleep deprivation, stress positions, waterboarding, sensory deprivation, electric shock, exposure to extreme heat and cold, and lack of adequate nutrition (Kurnaz, 2008). Is the use of these techniques justified in order to combat terrorism?

Case 10.5: Enhanced interrogation/torture
Consider the systems of ethics explored in Chapter 2 (religion, natural law, Utilitarianism, Ethics of Care, Ethical Egoism, and Ethical Formalism). Does enhanced interrogation serve society within the context of the ethical systems discussed in Chapter 2?

The International Criminal Court

Beginning in 1948, the concept of having an **ICC** was first broached by the UN. The UN International Law Commission drafted statutes in the 1950s that would establish an **ICC**, but the UN General Assembly rejected the creation of an **ICC** at that time. It wasn't until the 1990s that a conference was held in Rome, referred to as the **Rome Conference**, and the UN returned to the task of creating an **ICC**. This time, however, support for an **ICC** was largely precipitated by ad hoc tribunals for atrocities committed in both Rwanda and Yugoslavia exemplifying the need for a criminal court to address violations of **IHL**. In July 1998 the Rome Statute establishing an **ICC** passed and in April 2002 the minimum threshold of 60 member states officially ratifying and establishing the ICC was met. (Leonard, 2007)

The ICC's jurisdiction is based on whether a nation state is a member of the ICC and the nature of the **IHL** violation. Non-member states can also come under the **ICC**'s jurisdiction, but the **ICC** must seek approval from the UN in those instances. This makes the ICC's jurisdiction neither **universal jurisdiction**, applying to all states regardless of membership, nor is it **inherent jurisdiction**, allowing the prosecutor for the **ICC** the power to charge a state of crimes without seeking further approval in all circumstances. The **ICC** does have the power to prosecute member states of genocide, crimes against humanity, and war crimes without further approval from any other source. As of 2019, there were 123 **ICC** member states who are subject to the **ICC**'s jurisdiction without having to involve the UN. The types of crimes that the **ICC** has jurisdiction over include **genocide**, **crimes against humanity**, **war crimes**, and **crimes of aggression**.

The **ICC** has jurisdiction over acts of **genocide** which are defined as:

> acts committed with intent to destroy, in whole or in part, a national, ethnical, racial, or religious group, as such:
>
> (a) Killing members of the group;
> (b) Causing serious bodily or mental harm to members of the group;
> (c) Deliberately inflicting on the group conditions of life calculated to bring about its physical destruction in whole or in part;
> (d) Imposing measures intended to prevent births within the group;
> (e) Forcibly transferring children of the group to another group.
>
> (Leonard, 2007)

The **ICC** can also prosecute "conspiracy to commit **genocide**, public incitement to commit **genocide**, attempted **genocide**, and complicity in **genocide**" (Leonard, 2007). There was a special convention on genocide in 1948, the Genocide Convention, and the language defining **genocide** was taken directly from that convention. The **Rome Convention** delegates unanimously agreed to the **genocide** language.

Genocide and **war crimes** could be considered the catalysts for the creation of the **ICC**. In 1994, almost one million people were murdered in Rwanda in the worst example of **genocide**. The UN was forced to rely on an ad hoc tribunal to prosecute the guilty parties. Also, during the 1990s, the former Yugoslavia engaged in what their President called "ethnic cleansing" of non-Serbian citizens which resulted in the loss of hundreds of thousands of lives and millions of refugees. Another ad hoc tribunal was created by the UN to address the atrocities (Leonard, 2007). It became increasingly clear that relying on ad hoc responses to complex and continuous violations of **IHL** was inadequate, thus laying the groundwork for the creation of the **ICC**.

The **Rome Convention** defines **crimes against humanity** broader than traditional **IHL** which limits such crimes to only those occurring during armed conflicts. This was an area of debate during the **Rome Convention** which resulted in the expansion of the **crimes against humanity** definition. The **ICC** has jurisdiction over **crimes against humanity** regardless of whether they occur during armed conflicts. Widespread or systematic attacks against a civilian population such as murder, enslavement, torture, rape, sexual slavery, apartheid, and other inhumane acts are included among others. Often if a state is committing **genocide**, then they are also committing **crimes against humanity**, but the two types of crimes are not synonymous.

War Crimes are similar violations of **IHL** which occur during international armed conflict rather than during internal conflict within a state. After World War I, there was a movement to create a war crimes tribunal that was unsuccessful, however, the Nuremberg and Tokyo war crime tribunals post World War II were successful which paved the way for the **ICC**. **War crimes** include such acts as killing, torture, destruction of property, taking hostages, targeting civilians, rape, sexual slavery, starvation, using poisonous weapons/gases, and unlawful deportation. After much debate during the **Rome Convention**, the use of nuclear weapons was intentionally left out of the **war crimes** definition.

The most contentious debates during the creation of the **ICC** surrounded defining **crimes of aggression**. The **ICC** cannot bring charges of aggression against a state without UN Security Council approval whereas prior approval is unnecessary against member states with the other three types of crimes. **Crimes of aggression** involve international armed conflict where an invasion or an attack occurs unprovoked in violation of the UN Charter. It includes bombardment, blockades, as well as relying on mercenaries in carrying out armed conflict.

The **ICC** receives referrals from member states and the UN Security Council, but it can initiative an investigation on its own. The Office of the Prosecutor handles the investigations with cooperation from member states. Once an arrest warrant is issued, it is up to the member states to help bring the suspect into custody which can be difficult if the suspect remains in a non-member state or visits a member state diplomatically. In 2023, the **ICC** had 17 open investigations and has 6 individuals in custody, some that were originally opened as early as 2004. Since its inception, the court has heard 31 cases (ICC, 2023). One criticism of the **ICC** is that most of the investigations occur in Africa suggesting that the **ICC** may be susceptible to political pressure from non-African nations.

Case 8.6: Kidnapping children
In March 2023, over 16,000 Ukrainian children were forcibly placed with Russian families under Vladimir Putin's authority. This is considered both genocide and a crime against humanity. The ICC issued a warrant for Vladimir Putin's arrest. It is the first time that the leader of a country that is a permanent member of the UN Security Council has ever been targeted by the ICC. Should the ICC be pursuing charges against the leader of a member of the UN Security Council? What are the potential repercussions should Putin be brought into custody?

Case 8.7: ICC punishments

Consider the various theories of punishment discussed in the previous chapter (retribution, incapacitation, deterrence both specific and general, rehabilitation, and restorative justice) with respect to the following ICC cases and which theory makes the most sense given the facts of the case:

1. From April 2012 to January 2013 Timbuktu, Mali was attacked and taken over by two terrorist groups - Ansar Dine and Al-Qaeda in the Islamic Maghreb (AQIM). Al Hassan Ag Mahmoud, who was a part of these attacks, was charged in 2019 with war crimes and crimes against humanity for taking over the residents of Timbuktu and using violence and torture to control every aspect of life. Al Hassan regularly arrested and sentenced residents without judicial proceedings, subjected Timbuktu citizens to torture and inhumane acts like amputating limbs and forcing women into acts of sexual slavery.

2. Germain Katanga was convicted of being an accessory in one crime against humanity and four war crimes by assisting the Ngiti militia in murdering and attacking, destroying property, and pillaging the citizens of Bogoro in the Democratic Republic of the Congo. Katanga was an intermediary between weapons and ammunition suppliers with the Ngiti militia who carried out the crimes in 2003. Katanga also helped with organizing and equipping the Ngiti militia, as well as providing logistical aid, but he was not convicted of being a principal as he did not appear to have power to give out orders with respect to any type of implementation or to punish any members of the Ngiti militia.

3. In 2012, Mr. Thomas Lubanga Dyilo was found guilty of crimes against humanity for recruiting and conscripting children under the age of 15 to take active part in armed conflict in the Democratic Republic of the Congo. 129 victims were allowed to participate in his trial.
(ICC, 2023)

Conclusion

Policing IHL worldwide is challenging considering that atrocities happen despite lessons learned from the Holocaust. Major superpower nations like Russia and the United States are not immune from engaging in violations of IHL. Unfortunately, the ICC is limited in terms of executing warrants and bringing perpetrators to justice, relying on member states to self-prosecute and help bring suspects into custody where possible. The ICC has shown, however, that it will not sit idly by without taking action despite these limitations. A documentary entitled *Prosecutor* (2011) highlights some of the work of the ICC.

Debate Topics for In-Class Discussion

1. Goverments should rely on enhanced interrogation in investigations
    a. *Pro* – enhanced interrogation techniques can be useful in preventing future terrorist events
    b. *Con* – enhanced interrogation is torture and is ineffective in garnering accurate intelligence
2. Charging Vladimir Putin under the ICC's jurisdiction
    a. *Pro* – no one is above the law and Putin must be held responsible for his illegal actions
    b. *Con* – arresting and convicting Putin could lead to the next world war

Terms

International Humanitarian Law (IHL)
Geneva Conventions
Torture
Enhanced interrogation
International Committee of the Red Cross (ICRC)
Just War Theory/Just War Tradition
Jus ad bellum
Jus ad bello
Torture Memos
International Criminal Court (ICC)
Rome Conference
Universal jurisdiction
inherent jurisdiction
Genocide
Crimes against humanity
War crimes
Crimes of aggression

References

Childress, J. F. (1978). Just-war theories: the bases, interrelations, priorities, and functions of their criteria. *Theological studies*, 39(3), 427-445.

Convention against Torture and Other Cruel, Inhuman or Degrading Treatment or Punishment. December 10, 1984. https://www.ohchr.org/en/instruments-mechanisms/instruments/convention-against-torture-and-other-cruel-inhuman-or-degrading

Crawford, N. C. (2003). Just war theory and the US counterterror war. *Perspectives on Politics, 1*(1), 5-25.

Humphrey, T. (1983). To perpetual peace: A philosophical sketch. In *Perpetual Peace and Other Essays on Politics, History and Morals.* Cambridge, Mass.: Hackett.

Hutchinson, B. (2023, October 19). Israel-Hamas conflict: Timeline and key developments. *ABC News*. https://abcnews.go.com/International/timeline-surprise-rocket-attack-hamas-israel/story?id=103816006

International Criminal Court (ICC). (2023, October 19). The Court Today. https://www.icc-cpi.int/sites/default/files/2023-10/TheCourtToday-Eng.pdf

Johnson, D. A., Mora, A., & Schmidt, A. (2016). The Strategic Costs of Torture: How" Enhanced Interrogation" Hurt America. *Foreign Affairs, 95*(5), 121-132.

Kennedy, R. (Director). (2007). *Ghosts of Abu Ghraib*. [Documentary Film]. HBO Documentary Films and Moxie Firecracker Films.

Kurnaz, M. (2008). *Five Years of My Life: An Innocent Man in Guantanamo Bay*. St. Martin's Press.

Leonard, E. K. (2007). *Establishing an International Criminal Court: The Emergence of a New Global Authority?*. Georgetown University. School of Foreign Service. Institute for the Study of Diplomacy.

Nordgren, L. F., McDonnell, M. H. M., & Loewenstein, G. (2011). What constitutes torture? Psychological impediments to an objective evaluation of enhanced interrogation tactics. *Psychological science*, 22(5), 689-694.

Smeulers, A., & Van Niekerk, S. (2009). Abu Ghraib and the War on Terror—a case against Donald Rumsfeld?. *Crime, Law and Social Change*, *51*, 327-349.

Stevens, B. (Director). (2011). *Prosecutor*. [Documentary Film]. Icarus Films.

Chapter 11
White Collar Crime and Corporate Misconduct

Chapter Objectives

1. Introduce students to the concept of white-collar crime.
2. Discuss various types of white-collar crime focusing on fraud and the impact it has on employees, consumers, and the economy.
3. Consider the impact that excessive executive compensation has on society.

Introduction

In 2001, one of the biggest energy companies in the world, Enron, filed for bankruptcy. The **Enron scandal**, consisting of accounting fraud and insider trading, eventually led to the **2002 Sarbanes-Oxley Act** placing restrictions on corporations regarding their accounting practices and record keeping. Enron engaged in a controversial accounting practice called **mark-to-market accounting** which allowed corporations to speculate future profits and treat those profits as actually existing on their balance sheets. This accounting practice allows a company to boost their profile and entice investors.

Enron abused **mark-to-market accounting** and also engaged in a **Ponzi scheme** where recent investor funds are used to pay off previous investor obligations. In the end, the people who paid were Enron employees who lost their jobs and their pensions. One Enron corporate executive, Cliff Baxter, committed suicide before testifying against Enron in 2002. A documentary entitled *Enron: The Smartest Guys in the Room* fully covers the Enron scandal.

The downfall of corporations such as Enron has led to many policy changes. Regardless of these changes, corporate misconduct continues to negatively impact society. But there are other types of criminal and unethical behaviors aside from corporate misconduct and accounting fraud to consider. This chapter considers a variety of what are considered white-collar crimes including accounting fraud, consumer fraud, and employee theft and embezzlement. We end the discussion with a look at the ethics of excessive executive compensation.

White-Collar Crime

White-collar crime has been around at least since the fourth century BC where **embezzlement** of public money by anyone working for the government was a crime. The Bible talks about practicing fairness and how cheating in consumer transactions is immoral while the Talmud also frowns upon raising the price of goods in an unjust manner. Sutherland, the father of Differential Association Theory (DAT) discussed in Chapter 3 of this text, first conceptualized **white-collar crime** and he defined it "as a crime committed by a person of respectability and high social status in the course of his occupation" excluding crimes like murder that are not a part of an individual's normal occupation (Sutherland, 1950, p.9).

Sutherland's definition has several flaws in that it includes whether a perpetrator's social status is relevant to whether they've committed a **white-collar crime**. And some scholars thought Sutherland's definition could be interpreted to include non-criminal violations normally dealt with by civil laws. Sutherland's definition is an **offender-based approach** focusing on characteristics of the person committing the **white-collar crime**. An **offense-based approach** to defining **white-collar crime** eliminates the offender's status and focuses on the crimes committed. According to Albanese (1995), **white-collar crime** includes acts like deception and **fraud** committed in the scope of employment by an individual or a corporation.

There are a wide range of federal and state crimes that fit the definition of white-collar offenses. **White-collar crimes** are divided into several categories including theft by deception, public administration crimes, and regulatory offenses. Local police departments regularly report offenses and there are three that are considered white-collar offenses – **embezzlement**, forgery, and **fraud**. Within the federal code there are many more including bribery, bank embezzlement, antitrust violations, securities fraud, and tax fraud to name just a few. At the heart of each of these types of white-collar crimes is deception or fraud coupled with economic gain. And both the offenders and victims of white-collar crimes have some differences from perpetrators of other types of crime and their victims.

The demographic for **white-collar offenders** is not surprising for crimes such as antitrust, bank embezzlement, false claims, lending and credit fraud, mail and wire fraud, and securities fraud. These offenders are primarily white men ranging in age from 35 to 56 years old. A majority of white-collar offenders commit only a few offenses while about a quarter commit criminal offenses persistently, regularly seeking out criminal opportunities. Only a very small percentage commit a wider variety of crimes similar to that of a non-white-collar perpetrator (Benson & Chio, 2019).

Victims of **white-collar crimes** vary depending on the crime. Employers are victims of employee theft and embezzlement while employees are victims of companies committing **fraud** like Enron causing the company to shut down and raid pension funds. Every day citizens are susceptible to **consumer fraud**, particularly the elderly and those less sophisticated, but also clients of companies committing **fraud**. In Norway over a six-year period there were over 400 **white-collar crime** convictions and almost a third of the victims were employers while over 15% were company clients (Gottschalk, 2019). According to the FBI, of the over 750,000 victims of various types of **fraud** in 2022, approximately 49% were between the ages of 35 to 64 years old.

Fraud has been around as long as humans have been committing crimes. It is generally associated with trickery of some sort. According to Black's Law Dictionary:

> **fraud** consists of some deceitful practice or willful device, resorted to with intent to deprive another of his right, or in some manner to do him an injury.

Broadly defined, **fraud** is at the heart of white-collar crimes and touches most people at some point during their lives whether it be theft inside or outside of the workplace, identity misappropriation, or consumer scams. According to the Federal Trade Commission (FTC) in 2022, consumers alone lost nearly $8.8 billion to fraudulent schemes including imposters, online shopping, prizes, sweepstakes, lotteries, business and job opportunities, and investments. This chapter focuses on a variety of types of fraud, although, what is covered here is by no means exhaustive of the never-ending varieties of frauds and schemes.

Case 11.1: Natural disaster fraud
Unfortunately, con artists abound in the wake of a natural disaster. One example is a Hurricane Katrina fraud scheme where a Florida resident created an online website for collecting donations that were never intended to end up helping the victims in Louisiana. He was able to raise nearly $40,000 in just a few days after the hurricane made landfall. The online payment service he was using suspected something wasn't right and worked with the FBI to eventually uncover the fraud. The FBI arrested the perpetrator and charged him with multiple counts of wire fraud. Considering the various theories of punishment laid out in Chapter 9 (retribution, incapacitation, deterrence, rehabilitation, restorative justice), which best serves society in dealing with fraudsters like the one described here?

Accounting Fraud

Accounting fraud is a broad term that encompasses a wide range of corporate **disclosure violations**. Corporations may fail to file required financial statements with the **Securities and Exchange Commission**

(SEC) or those financial statements may contain misstatements misrepresenting the financial status of the company. Some common violations include inflating revenues/earnings of the company, making false or misleading financial statements about future prospects of the company, and lack of internal controls allowing mismanagement of finances (Gerety & Lehn, 1997).

Relying on one of the Big Five accounting firms (e.g., KPMG, Ernst & Young) has historically been thought to be one mechanism for avoiding **accounting fraud** until Arthur Andersen, one of the Big Five, was found to have engaged in accounting fraud practices during the Enron scandal. Post Enron, however, relying on the Big Five is still considered a reliable practice for avoiding accounting fraudulent practices (Lennox & Pittman, 2008). **Forensic accounting** is a method of detecting accounting fraud that is sometimes accomplished using large-scale data mining techniques (Honigsberg, 2020; Sharma & Panigrahi, 2013). The press acting as a watchdog is also one way in which **accounting fraud** is initially detected (Miller, 2006).

The costs associated with **accounting fraud** are significant. Once a corporation is linked to financial misconduct, on average they lose almost a third of their value in the marketplace (Karpoff et al., 2008). As in the Enron case and other similar large **accounting fraud** examples, hundreds and sometimes thousands of employees lose their jobs when a corporation is forced to declare bankruptcy. Those employees who do not lose their jobs typically see about a 9% to 12% decline in their wages (Choi and Gipper, 2019). Financial misconduct also affects the broader economy considering the impact on investment activity, hiring, and allocation of resources that are disrupted by exposing a corporation's **accounting fraud** (Hutton et al., 2014; Yuan & Zhang, 2015; Kedia & Philippon, 2009).

The determinant behind anyone willing to risk engaging in fraudulent practices depends on rational choice theory (RCT) as discussed in Chapter 1 of this text. Individuals will weigh the benefits in terms of profits against the costs of being caught. Personal and behavioral characteristics are also explanative considering most individuals willing to commit financial misconduct are men who are overconfident and dishonest with narcissistic personalities (Schrand & Zechman, 2012; Loewen et al., 2013). Whether **accounting fraud** occurs is also dependent on some internal and external factors like the difficulty and/or cost involved in verifying the value of goods and services during audits. Also the auditor's conscientiousness in conducting the audit impacts whether **fraud** is detected.

Case 11.2: Inflating revenues

In 2023, Donald Trump faced accounting fraud charges in a New York civil trial. The Attorney General in New York charged Trump with inflating the valuations of his various investments

> to increase his net worth -- thereby bumping his ranking on Forbes list of the wealthiest Americans -- but also to obtain more favorable loans, guarantee lower insurance premiums, and satisfy loan conditions tied to his net worth. (Charalambous & Katersky, 2023)

Charging Trump with accounting fraud was controversial considering he is a former U.S. President. Not to mention that in these types of cases the executives, the accounting firms, the employees creating the valuations, and the Board of Directors each point the finger at one another as being responsible. Should Donald Trump be held responsible as the top executive? Does his former presidency and future candidacy have any bearing on whether he is held responsible? If he is found guilty, what would be an appropriate punishment considering the theories of punishment laid out in Chapter 9 (retribution, incapacitation, deterrence, rehabilitation, restorative justice) in terms of best serving society?

Consumer Fraud

There is a plethora of ways to defraud the general public. The FTC's 2017 Survey of Mass-Market Consumer Fraud asked questions about 19 different scams against the public. Some of these scams in the survey included the selling of fraudulent weight-loss products, fraudulent computer repairs, and being falsely told that you owe money to the government. There were also questions about a variety of unauthorized billing scams for a number of items like internet services, club memberships, and cellphone items.

Almost 16% of respondents equaling 40 million U.S. citizens answered that they had been victims at some point of at least one of the crimes presented in the survey over the previous year. Interestingly, fraudulent weight-loss products topped the list with 6.5 million respondents indicating they had been victims of this **consumer fraud** during the previous year. Fraudulent computer repair came in second with 5 million victims and falsely being told you owe money to the government rounded out third place with 3.4 million victims (Anderson, 2019).

Victims generally purchased fraudulent goods and/or services via the internet (62%) and over the telephone (26%). Victims first learn about fraudulent goods and/or services via the internet (54%) and in 12% of incidents the goods and/or services were promoted via social media and less than 3% of the time via email. Consumers paid $100 or more about 50% of the time when falling victim to a fraudulent scheme with the biggest individual losses happening with fraudulent business opportunities ($650 per victim) and credit repair ($350 per victim). Victims rely on credit and debit cards 75% of the time for making payments to fraudulent schemes (Anderson, 2019).

Generally, women are more likely to be victims of **consumer fraud** than men. Individuals with some college or technical school are also more likely to succumb to **consumer fraud**. African Americans and Hispanics are victims of **consumer fraud** at rates higher than non-Hispanic Whites. And individuals with a salary range of $36,000 to $60,000 have the highest incidence of victimization for **consumer fraud** (Anderson, 2019).

In terms of the personality of the victim, individuals who are more willing to take risks or who engage in risky purchasing practices are more likely to become victims of **consumer fraud**. Also, people who have recently experienced a serious negative life event are more likely to become victims of **consumer fraud**. With respect to financial stability, those who have more debt than they can currently handle are victimized at a higher rate. Those who have a much higher expected future income are also more likely to become a victim of **consumer fraud** (Anderson, 2019).

There are many agencies and workgroups tasked with fighting **consumer fraud**. Attorney Generals for each state typically have information available on their state-run websites about **consumer fraud** with easy mechanisms for consumers to report being victims of fraud or suspicious fraudulent schemes they may come across. The FTC has a Bureau of Consumer Protection that focuses on privacy and identity protection, advertising practices, financial practices, as well as a variety of other unfair and deceptive business tactics. There is also a Consumer Financial Protection Bureau focusing exclusively on banks, lenders, and financial institutions protecting the public from **consumer fraud**. And in 2018, then President Trump signed an executive order that established a task force for fighting **consumer fraud** and appointed the Deputy Attorney General as the chair.

In addition to these government resources there are also non-profit agencies that act as watchdogs protecting the public. One of the best known consumer advocates is Ralph Nader who uncovered problems in the auto industry that led to the manufacturing of unsafe vehicles in order to save company profits. Nader is also well known for his criticism of the FTC which eventually led to massive improvements in the agency's approach to protecting consumers. Despite these many governmental and non-governmental mechanisms for protecting consumers, fraud persists and continues to grow.

Case 11.3: Fraud via social media
Social media is seeing big increases in reports of marketing fraud for clothing and electronics, in particular. Facebook and Instagram are the most often utilized social media platforms for these types of scams. The largest losses for social media scams in terms of dollars are for fake investment opportunities. Social media scammers are capable of targeting their victims by reading their posts and hacking their accounts. There are even romance scams where a stranger will try to start a relationship via social media before asking for money from their victim. Naturally, the victims are much younger than typical consumer fraud victims with 47% between the ages of 18 to 19 years old and 38% between the ages of 20 to 29 (Fletcher, 2023). What can be done to catch these predators? How can we protect people from becoming victims? What should the punishment be considering the theories of punishment laid out in Chapter 9 (retribution, incapacitation, deterrence, rehabilitation, restorative justice) in terms of best serving society?

Case 11.4: The Ford Pinto
Perhaps one of Ford's biggest mistakes was its decision to value profit over safety in the 1970s with one of its subcompact cars they called the Pinto. Decisions were made regarding the placement of the fuel tank that led to the Pinto exploding when rear-ended resulting in some fatal accidents. Ford was sued with claims that they knew the fuel tank placement would cause fatalities while Ford argued that they were following industry standards and regulations. Should automakers be held responsible for deaths and/or damages that happen in car accidents? If so, what level of responsibility do they hold?

Employee Theft

Occupational fraud is any fraud that is committed by the people who work for a corporation including officers, directors, and employees (ACFE, 2018). The most common form of **occupational fraud** is **asset misappropriation**, or employee theft also referred to as embezzlement. The Association of Certified Fraud Examiners (ACFE) defines **asset misappropriation** as:

a scheme in which an employee steals or misuses the employing organization's resources (e.g., theft of company cash, false billing schemes, or inflated expense reports). (ACFE, 2018, p. 78)

Asset misappropriation makes up the highest percentage of **occupational fraud** while also being the least costly. Meanwhile, financial statement fraud is the least common but is the costliest type of **occupational fraud** (ACFE, 2018).

Of the types of **asset misappropriation**, check and payment tampering, billing, and noncash schemes make up the most expensive of the asset misappropriation schemes. Cash larceny, payroll, skimming, expense reimbursement, register disbursements, and cash on hand are next in line in terms of risks to organizations. The quicker the duration of the fraudulent scheme, the less costly that scheme is to an organization (ACFE, 2018). Fraudsters conceal their crimes using a variety of methods as indicated in Table 1 below.

Concealment Method	Efforts to Conceal
Created fraudulent physical documents	55%
Altered physical documents	48%
Created fraudulent transactions in the accounting system	42%
Altered transactions in the accounting system	34%
Altered electronic documents or files	31%
Destroyed physical documents	30%
Created fraudulent electronic documents or files	29%
Created fraudulent journal entries	27%

Table 11.1: *Fraudulent Concealment Tactics* (ACFE, 2018)

Occupational fraud is detected primarily through tips (40%), and more than half of those tips come from internal employees (53%). Almost a third of tips come from external sources like customers and outside vendors. The vast majority of frauds occur at for-profit companies with small businesses experiencing losses twice as much per scheme as compared to larger organizations. The highest median losses occur in communications and publishing ($525,000), energy organizations ($300,000), professional services ($258,000), and manufacturing organizations ($240,000). Interestingly, in 90% of cases where a background check was done on an employee who later engaged in fraud no red flags were revealed (ACFE, 2018).

Case 11.5: Employee theft
Imagine you are the manager confronted with an employee who is stealing from the company. What are your options for handling this type of situation? Consider the theories of punishment laid out in Chapter 9 (retribution, incapacitation, deterrence, rehabilitation, restorative justice) in terms of what best serves your company. Consider the following examples of employee theft that you would be faced with as manager: 1. One of your employees is voiding cash transactions at the register once they've collected the money from the customer and then pocketing the cash. This has been going on for several months and you have estimated that the employee has stolen approximately $2,000 from the company. 2. Your company hosts an annual fundraiser, and the donations are given to a local charity. One of your workers has been pocketing some of the cash donations and you estimate they've stolen approximately $500 this year alone. 3. One of your employees is overbilling customers and pocketing the extra money. This has been going on for over a year and you estimate that the employee has stolen approximately $15,000 this past year. 4. One employee has been forging payments by writing company checks to themselves and then creating fake entries to cover up these payments. This has been going on for over three years and you estimate the amount stolen exceeds $60,000.

Excessive Executive Compensation

The question of **excessive executive compensation** does not fall within the parameters of fraud necessarily unless it is achieved through some type of deception. The issue is whether executives are overcompensated for the work that they do. If the market requires executives to be highly compensated because there are far fewer senior managers who are all in demand, then there is an argument to pay them accordingly. Or where executive compensation can be linked to better corporate outcomes, then there may be no real moral dilemma.

Linking executive pay to corporate performance is virtually impossible to find (Jensen and Murphy, 1990; Tosi et al., 2000; van Essen et al., 2015; Aguinis et al., 2018). Executive pay also hurts shareholders (Ritholtz, 2017; Lownenstein, 2017; Karabell, 2018). And while some shareholders are able to push back on excessive executive compensation, many shareholders are either not in a position to speak up or are unable to speak up for a variety of reasons (Palmon et al., 2022). The wage gap between executives and the everyday employees who keep the company running perpetuates inequality within society. Does this seem a fair distribution of corporate resources?

The typical Chief Executive Officer (CEO) earns a compensation package that includes salary, benefits, bonuses, incentives, stocks, and stock options. The typical employee may not receive access to bonuses, incentives, stocks, or stock options depending on the corporation. Measuring the difference between executive and employee compensation is, therefore, a tricky affair. Despite these challenges, comparisons of executive compensation to employee compensation are quite startling. In 1965, the typical CEO was paid 21 times that of the typical employee as compared to 2022 where CEOs were paid 344 times that of the typical employee (Bivens & Kandra, 2023).

Case 11.6: Excessive executive compensation
The rise of union strikes in the United States in 2023 highlights the frustration that workers have with their lagging compensation. The actors and writers strikes along with the United Auto Workers all demanded better wages. While unions play an important role in bridging the wage gap, not all industries are unionized. And even after a successful strike, executive compensation may not be impacted. Should executive compensation be regulated? If so, how can executive compensation be controlled?

Conclusion

From 2007 through 2010 a global subprime mortgage crisis upended multiple national economies including within the United States. People lost jobs and housing while companies went bankrupt. The mortgage crisis also spurred recessions in several countries. This crisis was in part a result of lenders offering mortgages to higher risk clients at interest rates that increased, forcing consumers to walk away from their homes. During the crisis in the United States three of the largest investment banks went bankrupt and the banking industry had to be bailed out by the government. To date no individuals or organizations have been held responsible for the mortgage crisis despite the many failures of the banking industry. The mortgage crisis is an example of the impact questionable corporate tactics can have on consumers and society.

Debate Topics for In-Class Discussion

1. Harsh penalties for fraudsters
    a. *Pro* – both general and specific deterrence benefits with criminals who may be easier to deter
    b. *Con* – fraud is an economic harm, not a violent crime
2. Politicians who are accused of committing fraud should be forced to step down from public office
    a. *Pro* – no one is above the law and if there is enough to indict someone of fraud, then continuing to hold public office distracts from their duties to represent their district

b. *Con* – an indictment is not the same as a conviction which could lead to frivolous indictments for political gain

Terms

Enron scandal
Sarbanes-Oxley Act
Mark-to-market accounting
Ponzi scheme
White-collar crime
Embezzlement
Offender-based approach
Offense-based approach
Fraud
White-collar offenders
Consumer fraud
Accounting fraud
Disclosure violations
Securities and Exchange Commission (SEC)
Forensic accounting
Occupational fraud
Asset misappropriation
Excessive executive compensation

References

Aguinis, H., Gomez-Mejia, L. R., Martin, G. P., & Joo, H. (2018). CEO pay is indeed decoupled from CEO performance: Charting a path for the future. *Management Research: Journal of the Iberoamerican Academy of Management, 16*(1), 117-136.

Albanese, Jay S. (1995). *White-Collar Crime in America.* Englewood Cliffs, NJ: Prentice Hall.

Anderson, K. B. (2019). Mass-market consumer fraud in the United States: A 2017 update. *Federal Trade Commission.* Washington, DC.

Association of Certified Fraud Examiners (ACFE). (2018). *Report to the Nations. 2018 Global Study on Occupational Fraud and Abuse.*

Benson, M. and Chio, H. (2019). Who Commits Occupational Crimes? *The Handbook of White-Collar Crime,* 97-112.

Bivens, J., & Kandra, J. (2023, September 21). *CEO pay slightly declined in 2022*. Economic Policy Institute.

Black's Law Dictionary (2nd ed. 2023).

Charalambous, P., & Katersky, A. (2023, Oct. 17). *Trump set to return to the civil fraud trial that could threaten his business empire.* ABC News.

Choi, J., & Gipper, B. (2019). *Fraudulent financial reporting and the consequences for employees*. Research Paper No. 19-19, Stanford University Graduate School of Business, Stanford, CA.

Federal Trade Commission. (2023, Feb. 23). *New FTC Data Show Consumers Reported Losing Nearly $8.8 Billion to Scams in 2022*. [Press Release]. https://www.ftc.gov/news-events/news/press-releases/2023/02/new-ftc-data-show-consumers-reported-losing-nearly-88-billion-scams-2022

Fletcher, R. (2023, Oct. 6). *Social media: A golden goose for scammers.* Federal Trade Commission. [Data Spotlight]. https://www.ftc.gov/news-events/data-visualizations/data-spotlight/2023/10/social-media-golden-goose-scammers#3

Gerety, M., & Lehn, K. (1997). The causes and consequences of accounting fraud. *Managerial and Decision Economics, 18*(7-8), 587-599.

Gibney, A. (Director). (2005). *Enron: The Smartest Guys in the Room.* [Documentary Film]. Magnolia Films.

Gottschalk, P. (2019). Types of Harm, Extent of Harm, and the Victims of Occupational Crime. *The Handbook of White-Collar Crime*, 47-63.

Honigsberg, C. (2020). Forensic accounting. *Annual Review of Law and Social Science, 16*, 147-164.

Hutton, I., Peterson, D. R., & Smith, A. H. (2014). The effect of securities litigation on external financing. *Journal of Corporate Finance, 27*, 231-250.

Jensen, M. C., & Murphy, K. J. (1990). Performance pay and top-management incentives. *Journal of political economy, 98*(2), 225-264.

Karabell S. (2018, February 14). Executive compensation is out of control. What now? *Forbes*.

Karpoff, J. M., Lee, D. S., & Martin, G. S. (2008). The cost to firms of cooking the books. *Journal of financial and quantitative analysis, 43*(3), 581-611.

Kedia, S., & Philippon, T. (2009). The economics of fraudulent accounting. *The Review of Financial Studies, 22*(6), 2169-2199.

Lennox, C. S., & Pittman, J. (2008). Big five audits and accounting fraud. *Available at SSRN 1137829*.

Loewen, P. J., Dawes, C. T., Mazar, N., Johannesson, M., Koellinger, P., & Magnusson, P. K. (2013). The heritability of moral standards for everyday dishonesty. *Journal of Economic Behavior & Organization, 93*, 363-366.

Lownenstein, R. (2017, April 19). Breaking the CEO pay cycle. *Fortune*.

Miller, G. S. (2006). The press as a watchdog for accounting fraud. *Journal of Accounting Research, 44*(5), 1001-1033.

Palmon, D., Kleinman, G., & Medinets, A. F. (2022). Giving Shareholders Real Rights, Reducing Excessive Executive Pay, and Reducing One-Size-Fits-All Regulation. *Rutgers Business Review, 7*(3), 211-236.

Ritholtz, B. (2017, March 6). Excessive CEO pay for dumb luck. *Bloomberg*.

Schrand, C. M., & Zechman, S. L. (2012). Executive overconfidence and the slippery slope to financial misreporting. *Journal of Accounting and economics*, *53*(1-2), 311-329.

Sharma, A., & Panigrahi, P. K. (2013). A review of financial accounting fraud detection based on data mining techniques. *arXiv preprint arXiv:1309.3944*.

Sutherland, E. H. (1983). *White-Collar Crime: The Uncut Version.* New Haven: Yale University Press.

Sutherland, E. H. (1950). *White Collar Crime*. New York: Dryden Press.

Tosi, H. L., Werner, S., Katz, J. P., & Gomez-Mejia, L. R. (2000). How much does performance matter? A meta-analysis of CEO pay studies. *Journal of management*, *26*(2), 301-339.

Van Essen, M., Otten, J., & Carberry, E. J. (2015). Assessing managerial power theory: A meta-analytic approach to understanding the determinants of CEO compensation. *Journal of management*, *41*(1), 164-202.

Yuan, Q., & Zhang, Y. (2015). Do banks price litigation risk in debt contracting? Evidence from class action lawsuits. *Journal of Business Finance & Accounting, 42(9-10),* 1310-1340.

Chapter 12
Ethical Treatment of Juveniles

Chapter Objectives

1. Consider the ways in which juveniles are treated within the justice system.
2. Discuss the various mechanisms for intervening to help rehabilitate juveniles.
3. Explore the impact that abuse and neglect has and children.
4. Look at the role law enforcement officers play in school systems.

Introduction

In Bryan Stevenson's book, *Just Mercy*, there is a chapter about a 14-year-old boy named Charlie who ends up in an adult prison. George, Charlie's mother's abusive boyfriend, regularly abuses Charlie's mother and eventually Charlie shoots George for beating Charlie's mother unconscious. While in adult prison, Charlie is abused by the other incarcerated individuals, but eventually Stevenson becomes Charlie's lawyer. With Stevenson's help, once Charlie is released from prison he is able to pursue a college degree (Stevenson, 2015). It is a heartbreaking story, but one with a happy ending which seems rare in the justice system.

Charlie's story highlights the hope that with juveniles there is an opportunity to turn someone's life around. Juveniles who end up involved in the justice system typically come from traumatic backgrounds as seen in Charlie's case. This chapter focuses on the treatment of juveniles in both the juvenile justice system and the adult system. Other considerations include the use of boot camps and other non-traditional juvenile justice interventions, lengthy and/or harsh sentencing, the concept of incorrigibility, and the victimization of juveniles both inside and outside of the criminal justice system.

Treatment of Juveniles in the Justice System

Under the law, distinguishing between juveniles and adults is a controversial affair. Psychologists argue that brain development and subsequent social development in **juveniles** make it hard for them to make good decisions. It is evidenced by crime across the lifespan where many **juveniles** who commit petty crimes in their youth outgrow this behavior as their attachments and bonds to institutions and people mature. As such, the justice system is divided into **juvenile** and adult systems of courts and correctional institutions.

The problem is figuring out at what age is an individual capable of making sound decisions such that we can hold them accountable when they commit crime. This stems from the concept of **mens rea** under the criminal law. Every crime requires that the actor has met a minimum level of requisite intent in order to be charged and sometimes lack of that **mens rea** is enough to excuse the criminal behavior. Another example of lacking **mens rea** includes individuals who have a mental disease or defect that causes criminal behavior sometimes also coupled with an inability to understand that their behavior is, in fact, wrong which is the basis for an insanity defense.

Historically in the United States, **juveniles** were treated as adults in the system until the beginning of the 20th century. In some states but not all, treating **juveniles** as adults is typically reserved for violent crimes like murder, rape, and arson. States vary regarding where they draw the line for treating **juveniles** as adults. Minimum ages to try a **juvenile** as an adult vary with many states not specifying a minimum age. The most common minimum age for transferring to or charging a **juvenile** in the adult system is 14 years old (Snyder & Sickmund, 2006). Brain development, however, still categorizes adolescence as continuing through age 24 (Arain et al., 2013).

The issue of where to hold juveniles being processed in the adult system is also thorny considering how much more vulnerable juveniles are to becoming victims. And adult prisons lack programming specifically for juveniles considering their developmental needs. Over the last two decades, the number of **juveniles** being held in adult jails and prisons has fallen from a high of over 10,000 in 2009 to around 2,250 in 2021 which is a sign that the correctional system recognizes that adult facilities may not be the best option when it comes to **juveniles** (Zhen et al., 2023).

As was the case with Charlie, **juveniles** tend to be victimized easily by other incarcerated individuals in adult correctional facilities. The problem of rape in correctional facilities has been so prevalent that in 2003 Congress passed the **Prison Rape Elimination Act (PREA)** which included creating a commission to investigate the problem. The commission's report recognized that **juveniles** were more at risk than any other group from rape victimization in correctional facilities (PREA Commission Report, 2009). While juvenile detention facilities also have problems with protecting juveniles from abuses by corrections staff and from abusing one another, they remain a better alternative than adult correctional facilities.

Case 12.1: Age and nature of the offense
At what age should we hold juveniles accountable for their criminogenic behaviors? What about the individual development of the perpetrator? How should we factor in the seriousness of the offense? Consider the following real examples and the age one should be held accountable: 1. A 17-year-old turning 18 in just a couple of months and driving 95 miles per hour with a blood alcohol content of 0.08% crashed into another car killing the driver. 2. Michael, a 13-year-old, who comes from a troubled family and was living on the street at the age of 11, is set up by adults (who think because he's a juvenile he'll get a lesser sentence) to shoot and kill a 23 year old man in front of his wife and two children 3. A 16-year-old accused of three carjackings, a kidnapping, and seven robberies all within a short time-span of a couple of weeks.

Non-Traditional Juvenile Justice Interventions

As an alternative to traditional jails, prisons, and juvenile detention facilities, **boot camps** provide a structured environment that is modeled after military boot camps. Since the early 1980s, courts across the United States have relied on these programs first for adults and then eventually also for **juveniles**. The programming focuses primarily on physical activity and training-type drills where the participants have their hair shaved, wear uniforms, and have a graduation ceremony at the completion of their programming, thus mirroring the military boot camp experience (Mackenzie & Hebert, 1996).

Juvenile boot camps tend to have less harsh labor as required by law. They also provide academic programming which is also a legal requirement. Where some of these programs differ, however, is in the amount of therapeutic treatment provided to the participants. Boot camps receive mixed results in terms of effectiveness across the board. However, at least one meta-analysis has shown that those programs offering therapeutic treatment tend to have lower recidivism rates for participants who graduate from their programs (Wilson et al., 2005).

Some studies of **faith-based programming** in correctional settings have found a variety of positive outcomes in terms of incarcerated individuals attaining self-improvement (Clear & Sumter, 2013; O'Connor & Perreyclear, 2013; Johnson et al., 2002). There is not much research in this area, but theory suggests strong bonds with prosocial institutions can cut down on criminogenic behaviors. Funding these programs is difficult considering the separation of church and state in the United States. And **juveniles** who are atheist can be left out of any programing sponsored by religious organizations (Cox & Matthews, 2007).

Juvenile drug treatment diversion courts have significantly lower recidivism rates for their graduates than those juveniles who do not complete their programs (Stein et al., 2013). Although, **juveniles** who engage in intervention programs and who have committed more serious crimes (e.g., sexual, violent) have bigger reductions in recidivism than those who have committed less serious crimes (e.g., drug) (Pappas & Dent, 2023). One problem is finding rehabilitative treatment programs that will accept **juveniles**. Out-patient programs are easier to come by, but in-patient facilities are more reluctant to accept **juveniles** and are particularly sensitive to accepting **juveniles** with significant mental health problems.

Significant **juvenile mental health problems** can lead to involvement in the juvenile justice system. And one issue that plagues youths in society is access to adequate mental health services. Congress and many states continually work to pass legislation increasing access to mental health care for children in schools which is helpful (DHHS, 2021). However, even with these efforts, not all children in need of mental health services receive those services. One meta-analysis found across various sectors that not all youth who need those services are actually receiving them (Duong et al., 2021). In general, youth find access to mental health services in a variety of institutions as evidenced in Table 12.1 below.

Sector	Receiving care	Elevated mental health symptoms/diagnoses care
School mental health services	7.28%	22.10%
Outpatient settings	7.26%	20.56%
Primary care	1.76%	9.93%
Inpatient	1.80%	9.05%
Child welfare	1.35%	7.90%
Juvenile justice	0.90%	4.50%

Table 12.1: *Youth in Need of Mental Health Care in the United States* (Duong et al., 2021)

One area of juvenile intervention that has gotten a lot of attention over the last couple of decades is **adventure-based programming (ABP)** for at-risk youth; sometimes also referred to as wilderness programs. Outward Bound is probably the best example of **ABP** for at-risk youth, being the first established in the early 1940s. Since that time, a number of programs have emerged to engage at-risk youth before they become involved with the justice system. Programing focuses on a variety of skills including physical activity, academic, communication, team building, socializing, and self-care.

For example, one **ABP** brings sixth, seventh, and eighth graders to a nature preserve regularly over a 15-week period during the school year. The activities that the children engage in include hiking, camping, rope climbing, and hands-on educational activities. Participants in the program experienced increased self-confidence, school attachment, resiliency, and an increase in maturity (Merenda, 2021). Other studies have similarly found potential for youth self-improvement in these programs including communication, leadership, positive attitudes, self-esteem, and team building (Deane & Harré, 2014).

Case 12.2: Boot camp
Some studies show that at-risk youths and juveniles respond well to boot camp environments while some juveniles report not connecting with these types of programs. Imagine that you are a judge overseeing a juvenile delinquency court. Would you consider sending defendants to a boot camp environment as a part of their sentencing? What would you require of the program in order to feel comfortable sentencing a juvenile to that program? What would you do with the juvenile if they were unable to complete the program?

Case 12.3: Religious programming for juveniles
While studies show the many benefits of both adults and youth connecting with prosocial institutions like religious organizations, it is relatively unclear the impact these programs have on juveniles. Imagine you are a judge who sentences juveniles regularly to non-traditional camps that help rehabilitate troubled youth. If the camps you rely on required participants to pray and/or attend religious services on Sunday would this impact your decision? What if the camp doesn't require prayer or religious services, but is run by a religious organization where voluntary prayer and religious services are offered at the camp – would you sentence juveniles to this type of programming?

Incorrigibility and Harsh Sentencing

The concept of **incorrigibility** is a legal one that applies specifically to **juveniles**. Incorrigibility exists when a juvenile offender has shown a pattern of criminogenic behavior suggesting that the youth is incapable of changing. According to Justice Kagan, it is a determination that a juvenile offender will remain dangerous in society forever (*Miller v. Alabama*, 2012). However, U.S. jurisprudence appears to reject this notion to some extent.

In ***Roper v. Simmons*** (2005), the U.S. Supreme Court held that a 17-year-old could not receive the death penalty in a capital case as it constituted cruel and unusual punishment under Eighth and Fourteenth Amendment. The Court expanded their protections to **juveniles** in ***Graham v. Florida*** (2010) finding that sentencing a 16-year-old to **life without the possibility of parole** (LWOP) in a non-homicide case also constituted cruel and unusual punishment under the Eighth and Fourteenth Amendments. Later, in ***Miller v. Alabama*** (2012), the Court held that sentencing a 14-year-old on a homicide conviction to life without the possibility of parole is cruel and unusual punishment under the Constitution.

The concept that youth could be **incorrigible** does have support in the research. Recidivism for convicted homicide offenders is higher than that of non-murderers (Broadhurst et al., 2018; Liem, 2013). And juveniles who have committed murder recidivate at high levels in committing additional murders (DeLisi et al., 2019). Interventions, including behavioral interventions, for youth who have been labeled **incorrigible** have mixed results with medications showing the most promise over traditional behavioral treatments (Haerle, 2019; Asscher et al., 2018; Butler et al., 2021).

This leaves us with the question of what punishments are appropriate for juveniles, particularly those committing violent offenses, and those who repeatedly commit violent offenses. Within the framework of life sentencing, there are also options to sentence an offender to **life with the possibility of parole** (LWP) or **LWP** after a statutory designated period of time. These sentences while giving hope to the offender can also be quite lengthy and even extend beyond the life expectancy of the offender. And even with the hope of release, parole boards tend to be reluctant to release offenders, can be unpredictable, and may not all consider the same factors when making decisions (Kokkalera & Singer, 2023).

Case 12.4: Sentencing juveniles for violent offenses
Juveniles who end up in the justice system, regardless of whether they are labeled as incorrigible, typically come from broken homes where they were neglected facing daily trauma. Does it make sense to sentence juveniles to lengthy sentences in any circumstances? Which offenses would you consider sentencing a juvenile to a life-type sentence? How would you determine the likelihood of rehabilitating any given juvenile offender? Do you believe that there are just some juveniles who are incorrigible and beyond changing?

Case 12.5: Parole decisions

When he was 13-years-old, Eric was convicted for murdering a four-year-old. Imagine you are a member of the parole board. This is what Eric says during his hearing:

> [H]e didn't deserve anything that I did to him, and no-one [sic] deserved that kind of violence or any kind of violence of that nature . . . [Y]ou can't justify something like that and I'm not going to even try. What I can tell you is that at the time, I had no value system towards life. I didn't value life. . . . I took my anger and frustration and rage out on him . . . .
> (Sloan, 2015)

Eric also talks about how he had been bullied growing up. He discusses everything that he's accomplished in prison including getting his GED, getting certified in carpentry and electrical work, and participating in therapy. Eric has not received any type of discipline in the past 10 years of his 20-year incarceration. He has plans for housing and a job. What is your decision regarding Eric? What factors did you take into consideration in making your decision?

Victimization of Juveniles in Society

While every state defines **abuse and neglect** by statute and sets its own standards for protecting children, the federal government defines it as:

> Any recent act or failure to act on the part of a parent or caretaker which results in death, serious physical or emotional harm, sexual abuse or exploitation; or an act or failure to act, which presents an imminent risk of serious harm.
> (CAPTA, 2010)

Abuse and neglect cases cause trauma for children that can eventually drive them to criminogenic behaviors. Tracking, identifying, intervening, and preventing abuse and neglect falls under the charge of **Child Protective Services (CPS)** agencies across the United States. Their mandate is to investigate cases of suspected **abuse and neglect**, place children in a safe environment including family care where a family member is willing to accept care for the children, approved foster care families, or approved group homes also known as orphanages.

CPS estimated that in 2021 alone they saw almost four million referrals of **abuse and neglect** for over seven million children which amounts to almost 3% of children nationwide. A little more than half of the referrals warrant an investigation. It is estimated that 1,820 children died from either abuse or neglect with the rates of child fatality for African American children being three times greater than that of white children and almost four times greater than Hispanic children (DHHS, 2023).

The youngest children, under the age of one-year-old, make up the largest percentage of **abuse and neglect** cases at over 25% with percentages steadily declining as children age. Caregivers who abuse alcohol or drugs, or those who have problems with finances and/or housing are at greater risk of abusing children. The highest prevalence of perpetrators is between the ages of 25 to 34 years old. Types of abuse include neglect, physical abuse, psychological maltreatment, sexual abuse, and sex trafficking (DHHS, 2023).

The goal of **CPS** is typically reunification of the child(ren) with the parent. Once the child(ren) is/are removed and put in a safe home environment, the parent can work towards **reunification**. During this time the parent receives **supervised visitation** until they are ready for less oversight and eventually visitation without any supervision by CPS caseworkers. Parenting education of some type can also be mandated by the judge as a term towards reunification.

In cases where the parent has a drug or alcohol problem, they can also be referred to a drug treatment diversion program specifically for abuse and neglect cases typically called **Family Drug/Treatment Court**. This type of treatment court is usually a civil court process and not a criminal court diversion, but judges can still in some circumstances use jail as a sanction for non-compliance. If **reunification** is not possible within a reasonable amount of time, then **CPS** can pursue what is called

permanency – a permanent, stable family environment through either existing extended family or adoption via the foster care system.

Another factor impacting juvenile delinquency is what has become known as the **school to prison pipeline**. Schools that rely on law enforcement, in particular **School Resource Officers (SRO)**, to control safety rather than relying on internal disciplinary measures can increase arrests of juveniles. School districts began turning more regularly to the use of **SROs** in the 1990s as a response to increases in violence on school property.

There is a big difference in a child's life, however, when making an arrest as opposed to subjecting the student to traditional disciplinary measures. Children who are arrested tend to drop out of school at younger ages and tend to get stuck in the revolving cycle of the justice system (Hjalmarsson, 2008; Aizer & Doyle, 2015). They also are much less likely to go to college which inhibits their job prospects (Lovenheim & Owens, 2014; Western, 2006). The positive side of having **SROs** is increases in safety for the school in terms of increases in arrests for violent offenses and drug charges (Owens, 2017).

Case 12.6: Permanency
Sarah has had her children removed for neglect and has been referred to a Family Treatment Court. Sarah's children are being taken care of by a family member while she works on getting sober. During her time in the treatment court, she realizes that she is struggling with staying sober and following all the rules of the treatment court. Eventually she decides she wants to give up and have her children permanently placed with the family member still caring for them. If you were the judge, what would you do?

Conclusion

In 2021, a 15-year-old Michigan high school student was charged with murdering four of his classmates at school. These types of cases make it challenging to convince the public that not holding juveniles to the same standards as adults in violent crimes is a good idea. Thinking back to those theories of punishment in Chapter 9, the more serious the crime, the more harm to a victim, the more difficult it is to advocate for rehabilitation or restorative justice. This chapter has tried to address the myriad of issues that arise when facing how juveniles enter and are ultimately treated within the justice system.

Debate Topics for In-Class Discussion

1. Juveniles should not be tried as adults
   a. *Pro* – protects children whose brains have not developed and provides more opportunities for rehabilitation
   b. *Con* – allows violent juveniles to avoid harsher punishments and culpability
2. Schools should not have SROs
   a. *Pro* – has a positive impact on the school to prison pipeline
   b. *Con* – makes schools less safe

Terms

Juveniles
mens rea
Prison Rape Elimaination Act (PREA)
Juvenile boot camps
Faith-based programming
Juvenile drug treatment diversion courts
Juvenile mental health problems
Adventure-based programming (ABP)
Incorrigibility
Roper v. Simmons
Graham v. Florida
Life without the possibility of parole (LWOP)
Miller v. Alabama
Life with the possibility of parole (LWP)
Abuse and neglect
Child Protective Services (CPS)
Reunification
Supervised visitation
Family Drug/Treatment Court
Permanency
School to prison pipeline
School Resource Officer (SRO)

References

Aizer, A., & Doyle Jr, J. J. (2015). Juvenile incarceration, human capital, and future crime: Evidence from randomly assigned judges. *The Quarterly Journal of Economics, 130*(2), 759-803.

Arain, M., Haque, M., Johal, L., Mathur, P., Nel, W., Rais, A., Sandhu, R., & Sharma, S. (2013). Maturation of the adolescent brain. *Neuropsychiatric disease and treatment, 9*, 449–461.

Asscher, J. J., Dekovic, M., Van den Akker, A. L., Prins, P. J., & Van der Laan, P. H. (2018). Do extremely violent juveniles respond differently to treatment? *International Journal of Offender Therapy and Comparative Criminology, 62*(4), 958–977.

Broadhurst, R., Maller, R., Maller, M., & Bouhours, B. (2018). The recidivism of homicide offenders in Western Australia. *Australian & New Zealand Journal of Criminology*, 51(3), 395–411.

Butler, H. D., Caudill, J. W., Craig, J. M., DeLisi, M., & Trulson, C. R. (2021). 99 percenters: An examination of the misconduct careers of the most violent and disruptive incarcerated delinquents. *Aggression and Violent Behavior, 60*, 101520.

Child Abuse Prevention and Treatment Act (CAPTA). 42 USC 5101. (2010).

Clear, T. R., & Sumter, M. T. (2013). *Prisoners, prison, and religion: Religion and adjustment to prison.* In Religion, the community, and the rehabilitation of criminal offenders (pp. 127-158). Routledge.

Cox, M., & Matthews, B. (2007). Faith-based approaches for controlling the delinquency of juvenile offenders. *Fed. Probation*, 71, 31.

Deane, K. L., & Harré, N. (2014). The youth adventure programming model. *Journal of Research on Adolescence, 24*(2), 293-308.

DeLisi, M., Bunga, R., Heirigs, M. H., Erickson, J. H., & Hochstetler, A. (2019). The past is prologue: Criminal specialization continuity in the delinquent career. *Youth Violence and Juvenile Justice*, 17(4), 335–353.

Duong, M. T., Bruns, E. J., Lee, K., Cox, S., Coifman, J., Mayworm, A., & Lyon, A. R. (2021). Rates of mental health service utilization by children and adolescents in schools and other common service settings: A systematic review and meta-analysis. *Administration and Policy in Mental Health and Mental Health Services Research, 48*, 420-439.

Graham v. Florida, 560 U.S. 48 (2010).

Haerle, D. R. (2019). Unpacking adultification: Institutional experiences and misconduct of adult court and juvenile court youth living under the same roof. *International journal of offender therapy and comparative criminology, 63*(5), 663-693.

Hjalmarsson, R. (2008). Criminal justice involvement and high school completion. *Journal of Urban Economics, 63*(2), 613-630.

Johnson, B. R., Tompkins, R. B., & Webb, D. (2002). Objective hope. *Philadelphia: Center for Research on Religion and Urban Civil Society.*

Kokkalera, S. S., & Singer, S. I. (2023). Now with the possibility of parole: Enabling a juvenile lifer's meaningful review. *The British Journal of Criminology, 63*(1), 115-133.

Liem, M. (2013). Homicide offender recidivism: A review of the literature. Aggression and Violent Behavior, 18(1), 19–25.

Lovenheim, M. F., & Owens, E. G. (2014). Does federal financial aid affect college enrollment? Evidence from drug offenders and the Higher Education Act of 1998. *Journal of Urban Economics, 81*, 1-13.

MacKenzie, D. L., & Hebert, E. E. (Eds.). (1996). *Correctional boot camps: A tough intermediate sanction.* DIANE Publishing.

Merenda, F. (2021). Adventure-Based Programming with at-Risk Youth: Impact upon Self-Confidence and School Attachment. *Child & Youth Services, 42*(4), 321-348.

Miller v. Alabama, 567 U.S. 460 (2012)

O'Connor, T. P., & Perreyclear, M. (2013). Prison religion in action and its influence on offender rehabilitation. In *Religion, the community, and the rehabilitation of criminal offenders* (pp. 11-33). Routledge.

Owens, E. G. (2017). Testing the school-to-prison pipeline. *Journal of Policy Analysis and Management, 36*(1), 11-37.

Pappas, L. N., & Dent, A. L. (2023). The 40-year debate: a meta-review on what works for juvenile offenders. *Journal of Experimental Criminology, 19*(1), 1-30.

Roper v. Simmons, 543 U.S. 551 (2005).

Sloan, S. (2015). Why Parole Eligibility Isn't Enough: What Roper, Graham, and Miller Mean for Juvenile Offenders and Parole. *Colum. Hum. Rts. L. Rev., 47*, 243.

Snyder, H. N. & Sickmund, M. (2006). *Juvenile offenders and victims: 2006 national report*. Washington, DC: U.S. Department of Justice, Office of Justice Programs, Office of Juvenile Justice and Delinquency Prevention.

Stein, D. M., Deberard, S., & Homan, K. (2013). Predicting success and failure in juvenile drug treatment court: A meta-analytic review. *Journal of substance abuse treatment, 44*(2), 159-168.

Stevenson, B. (2015). *Just mercy: A story of justice and redemption*. One World.

United States (PREA Commision Report) (2009). *National Prison Rape Elimination Commission Report*. Washington, DC: National Prison Rape Elimination Commission.

U.S. Department of Health & Human Services, Administration for Children and Families, Administration on Children, Youth and Families, Children's Bureau. (2023). *Child Maltreatment 2021*.

Western, B. (2006). *Punishment and inequality in America*. Russell Sage Foundation.

Wilson, D. B., MacKenzie, D. L., & Mitchell, F. N. (2005). Effects of correctional boot camps on offending. *Campbell Systematic Reviews, 1*(1), 1-45.

Zhen, Z., Carson, A., & Kluckow, R. (2023). Juveniles incarcerated in U.S. adult jails and prisons, 2002-2021. *Bureau of Justice Statistics.*

www.ingramcontent.com/pod-product-compliance
Lightning Source LLC
LaVergne TN
LVHW101505200926
848483LV00001B/228